D0560286

DATE DUE

A-10318

William McKinley

25th President of the United States

William McKinley, the 25th President of the United States, in his White House office. (Library of Congress.)

William McKinley

25th President of the United States

David R. Collins

 GARRETT EDUCATIONAL CORPORATION

Copyright © 1990 by David R. Collins

Manufactured in the United States of America

Edited and produced by Synthegraphics Corporation

Library of Congress Cataloging in Publication Data

Collins, David R.
  William McKinley, 25th president of the United States / David R. Collins.
     p.   cm. — (Presidents of the United States)
  Includes bibliographical references.
  Summary: Presents the life of William McKinley, including his childhood, education, employment, and political career.
  1. McKinley, William, 1843–1901 — Juvenile literature.
2. Presidents — United States — Biography — Juvenile literature.
3. United States — Politics and government —
1897–1901 — Juvenile literature.   [1. McKinley, William, 1843–1901.   2. Presidents.]
I. Title.   II. Title: William McKinley, twenty-fifth president of the United States.   III. Series.
E711.6.C65   1990
973.8′8′092 — dc20
[B]
[92]
ISBN 0-944483-55-0   89-39954
                                                                CIP
                                                                 AC

Contents

Chronology for William McKinley

1843 Born on January 29 in Niles, Ohio

1852– Attended public school and Poland
1860 Academy in Poland, Ohio

1860 Attended Allegheny College for less than a year

1860– Taught school; clerked in post office in
1861 Poland, Ohio

1861– Served in Union Army during the Civil
1865 War, rising from private to major

1865– Clerked in law office in Youngstown,
1867 Ohio; attended law school in Albany, New York

1867 Admitted to the Ohio bar; opened a law office in Canton, Ohio

1869 Elected prosecuting attorney of Stark County, Ohio

1871 Married Ida Saxton on January 25

1877– Served in the United States House of
1891 Representatives

1891 Elected governor of Ohio

1896 Elected 25th President of the United States

1900 Re-elected to a second term as President

1901 Shot by Leon Czolgosz on September 6 in Buffalo, New York; died on September 14

Chapter 1

Bloodshed in Buffalo

Once again, George Cortelyou carefully studied the papers spread over his desk. He was worried. As personal secretary to President William McKinley, Cortelyou was responsible for checking and doublechecking all of the chief executive's plans and appointments. It was a never-ending job, and a thankless one, too. People who were accommodated seemed to take it for granted, while those who were not were quick to anger. More than once he had incurred the wrath of a fuming, swearing senator or a disgruntled, insulted ambassador. It all went with the job.

As for McKinley, he relished the role of being a popular "people's President," always reaching for the nearest hand to shake or a baby's forehead to kiss. McKinley's methods had won him the heart of America's citizens, as well as their votes, and the personal concern of his secretary seemed to matter very little.

PLANNING A RECEPTION

Most of the arrangements for the President's visit to Buffalo, New York, were fine. The Pan-American Exposition of 1901 promised to be a perfect event for President McKinley as he slipped comfortably into his second term of office. He was eager to spotlight the ever-expanding trade agreements inno-

1

vated by the United States, thus promoting the nation as a commercial world power. The exposition promised to attract many leaders from Central and South America. Well aware of his own personal magnetism, McKinley welcomed the chance to "press the flesh" and meet eyeball to eyeball with businessmen outside the country's borders.

Cortelyou understood the purpose of McKinley's trip and found most of the plans satisfactory. The fireworks display, the sidetrip to Niagara Falls, the street parade through Buffalo—all were carefully charted and appeared to be reasonably safe. It was the reception at the Temple of Music that bothered the secretary. Ordinarily, a stream of people moving along a receiving line would not pose a major concern. But these were not ordinary times.

Recently, in countries around the world, anarchy was being preached. Anarchists (those who dislike any form of governmental authority) were threatening to overthrow governments with any means needed. Often such means were violent; most recently in Italy, a prime minister had been assassinated. Indeed, these were not the best of times for national leaders, and just the thought of such a thing happening in the United States caused George Cortelyou to break out in a cold, clammy sweat. The reception was simply too big a risk.

The cautious secretary sent word to John Milburn, the Buffalo attorney who was president of the Pan-American Exposition and who would serve as the President's host, that all plans were acceptable except for the reception on September 6 at the Temple of Music. That event was not acceptable.

But when McKinley learned of the cancelled reception, he rescheduled it. It was as much a personal decision as a political one. Not long after his second inauguration as President on March 4, Mrs. McKinley had taken ill. She was a chronic invalid who suffered from epilepsy, a brain disorder.

The President was accustomed to her extended sick spells, but this time she was especially slow in regaining her strength.

To avoid the summer heat, the McKinleys left Washington and spent most of the hot, sticky season in their Canton, Ohio, home. The change seemed to help, and by August Mrs. McKinley announced that she felt well enough to travel. The trip to Buffalo on September 4 to 6 sounded like fun, especially with the side jaunt to Niagara Falls, a trip the McKinleys had always planned to take but never had. Milburn's invitation seemed to be "just what the doctor ordered." When Cortelyou restated his objection to the reception at the Temple of Music, the chief executive simply shook his head.

"George, my friend," McKinley offered, exuding the warmth and charm so well practiced from years of successfully handling those who differed with him, "why should we call it off? No one would want to hurt *me*."

A POPULAR PRESIDENT

It certainly seemed that no one would want to hurt McKinley. To those who controlled America's big industries, his policy toward business was clear and simple: "Prices are fixed with a mathematical precision by supply and demand." The days of protecting national interests through high tariffs (taxes on imported goods) were over; now the emphasis was on open economic competition. It seemed an effective way to run a nation embarking on a new century.

But it was not just the big businessmen who had been won over by the man in the White House. He had not been born to wealth and power; what he had achieved had been through hard work and honest dedication. City worker and farmer alike heard his voice and listened to his "Bits of Wisdom" and "Daily Thoughts," as they appeared in the media.

His thinking reflected their own—rich with values and respect for the home. Some even called him "Papa McKinley," or "the old man," with a reverent tone in their voices.

McKinley enjoyed any opportunity to meet with the public personally, despite the objections of his concerned personal secretary. The President prided himself on the number of people he could shake hands with at any time, a conservative estimate being 50 a minute. An hour-long reception in the Temple of Music would allow him to greet 3,000 guests. No, McKinley stood firm on the matter; the visit to the Pan-American exposition in Buffalo would be carried out as originally planned, including the reception.

Arriving at dusk on the evening of Wednesday, September 4, the presidential train received a warm welcome by uniformed soldiers and a spirited marching band. Sounds of a 21-gun salute cracked through the air. One artillery lieutenant fired so close to the train that a car window shattered. Mrs. McKinley, startled and confused, fainted. Moments later, however, she regained consciousness and was ready to continue.

A Busy Day

Welcomed into the Milburn home, the McKinleys were offered every possible comfort. They retired early because the next day was going to be a busy one. It had been designated as President's Day, and the chief executive was scheduled to make a formal address. Attendance at the exposition had not been up to expectations, but it was hoped that 50,000 would visit the event on Thursday to see the President.

The hopes of the officials were realized. Attendance climbed well beyond the 50,000 mark. Certainly the fact that President William McKinley was speaking helped swell the numbers. As usual, the size of the crowd raised the chief executive's spirit; his voice resounded over the exposition grounds, drawing cheer after cheer as he spoke of reciprocal trade policies. "Isolation is no longer possible or desirable," the President thundered. He went on to declare the entire world a competitive marketplace, emphasizing that the United States would not only be a seller of goods, but a buyer as well. "If the quality and the price be right, of course we will purchase from other nations."

Aware that his remarks had pleased his audience, McKinley wore a smile and carried a laugh for the rest of the day. By contrast, a stern-looking George Cortelyou remained close to the chief executive, scrutinizing anyone and everyone nearby. The presidential party toured the exhibits, lunched at the New York State Building, and then continued visiting displays erected by foreign nations. That evening, the President and his wife enjoyed watching a fireworks display, climaxed by a pyrotechnic picture (one made of fireworks) of the country's leader blazing above the words, "Welcome to McKinley—Chief of our Nation." The day was a total triumph but exhausting as well, and the presidential party headed back to the Milburn home to rest before the final day at the exposition.

THE FATEFUL DAY

The last day of the President's visit to the exposition dawned bright and cheerful. For a fleeting moment, Cortelyou felt that he may have been foolish to have ordered an extra Secret Service man to accompany the presidential party. So far, all had gone beautifully. Glancing again at the day's schedule of events, the secretary grinned. New activities had been added to the crowded itinerary; the reception at the Temple of Music could last only 10 or 15 minutes. Good enough. The less time in that building, the better.

The morning excursion to Niagara Falls nearby offered McKinley a few hours of relaxation. There were meetings and social exchanges with local politicians and media people. But the visit also provided the President a chance to be with Mrs. McKinley—to cast aside official duties and merely enjoy the company of a loved one. Although a modest man in public, McKinley took his wife's hand as they spent several silent moments staring at the magnificent waterfalls. The Canadian side offered an even better view, and it would have taken but a short time to cross the International Bridge. However, McKinley knew that no U.S. President had ever left the country while still in office, and he did not want to be the first one to do so. He headed onto the bridge, scanned the sights as he walked, but carefully turned back before reaching the U.S.-Canadian border in the middle.

After a cold buffet lunch at the International Hotel, a visit to the powerhouse was scheduled. Dynamos and generators whirred loudly, but McKinley seemed oblivious to the noise. He was fascinated with all he witnessed, trying to understand the complicated aspects of how water produced electric power.

Following the visit to the powerhouse, it was back to Buffalo on the presidential train. While others in the party appeared a bit exhausted, McKinley looked fresh. As usual, he carried his top hat, its sleek coating gleaming in the afternoon sun. As the train rolled into Buffalo, Mrs. McKinley begged off attending the Temple of Music reception; she was tired, so no one encouraged her to change her mind. But matching her husband's earlier gesture of affection, she gently squeezed his hand before she left for the Milburn home.

With a little time to spare, the President's official party visited the Mission Building, where the Guatemalan Mirambon Quartet was performing. McKinley had a bite to eat while he visited with guests, clearly enjoying the rhythmic background music.

Gunshots in the Temple

By the time the presidential party arrived at the Temple of Music, all was in readiness. Most of the wooden chairs in the auditorium had been arranged to form a 10-foot-wide aisle for a short receiving line. People would enter the auditorium from the east and leave to the south. The Grand Marshal, Louis Babcock, had arranged for plenty of soldiers and guards to help keep order and the line moving. Nonetheless, George Cortelyou would be glad when the entire day was over. He stationed himself on President McKinley's right in the receiving line, with John Milburn on the chief executive's left in order to provide proper introductions as needed. Secret Service men were scattered close by.

As the east door was opened and the people began filing in, the sounds of a Bach sonata filled the air. The Temple of Music housed the biggest organ in the world, and organist William Gomph had looked forward to this moment for weeks. Carefully and with perfect precision, his hands played the multiple keyboards.

McKinley's hands moved with equal dexterity, warmly shaking each extended palm and smoothly moving the greeter on, all in the same motion. Not satisfied with the speed at which the crowd was moving, Babcock ordered the soldiers to move the people along more swiftly while Gomph was directed to increase the tempo of his music. More men and women crowded into the auditorium, wiping away the perspiration of the late afternoon heat with white handkerchiefs. Only McKinley seemed to remain untouched by the sticky temperature, always smiling his eternal smile. Cortelyou displayed no such composure. As the minutes ticked by, the secretary glanced nervously at his watch. He seldom looked into the faces of the people passing before him, but moved them toward the exit with barely a spoken word.

Then, at 4:07 P.M., it happened. A young man wearing

With his secretary, George Cortelyou, at his right, a stunned and wounded President McKinley faces Leon Czolgosz, a crazed anarchist who has just fired two bullets into the chief executive. (Library of Congress.)

a dark-gray suit, a string tie, and a flannel shirt reached the President. Around his right hand was a white handkerchief, appearing to cover an injury, yet lost among the many other similar linen cloths being used to dab sweat-covered foreheads. His smile ever congenial, McKinley reached for the stranger's hand. Without warning, the young man pushed the President's hand aside as he uncovered a revolver from his handkerchief-wrapped right hand and shoved it into McKinley's vest. Two muffled shots were fired, heard by those standing nearby. Cortelyou rushed forward as the President slipped against Milburn, while guards and Secret Service men wrestled the assailant to the floor.

"Cortelyou!" McKinley whispered, being helped into a nearby chair. "Cortelyou!"

The secretary leaned over his fallen leader, desperately trying to hear in the surrounding noise and confusion. It all seemed a ghastly nightmare as people stumbled and shouted. McKinley clutched his stomach as he began to realize what had just occurred. "My wife," he rasped. "Cortelyou, be careful how you tell her—oh, be careful." Cortelyou nodded, unable to speak and his eyes filling with tears. It was all so senseless, so utterly senseless. Nearby, soldiers pulled the attacker to his feet after retrieving the revolver. The scuffling caught the President's attention, and once more his kindly nature showed itself. "Go easy with him, boys," the injured McKinley ordered. "Don't hurt him."

A Nation Prays

Quickly the assailant was led to an office behind the stage while an ambulance was summoned for the wounded President. Guards cleared the area, with many people already fleeing the building. Most did not know exactly what had happened, only that McKinley had collapsed and the reception was over. By 4:18, the ambulance had deposited its passengers at the small exposition hospital. Regaining a bit of strength and recovering from the initial shock, the President turned to his secretary. "It must have been some misguided fellow," McKinley offered. Cortelyou merely nodded in agreement, helplessness and rage filling his thoughts.

A hurried examination revealed that two shots had been fired; the first merely bruised McKinley's lower ribs, while the second had entered his abdomen. Clearly an operation was in order, but no one wished to make the decision to go ahead. Once more, the duty fell upon Cortelyou. Upon seeking out all medical opinions present, the weary secretary gave his assent.

Meanwhile, news of the shooting quickly spread from Buffalo across the nation. There were rumors the President was dead, was injured, or had been miraculously saved. No one was certain what exactly had happened. But as the hours passed, the events of the afternoon were clarified. Yes, President William McKinley had been hit by at least one assassin's bullet. He was undergoing surgery in Buffalo and only time would tell just how serious the wounds were. Would he die? That question remained unanswered, seldom voiced but often pondered.

Everywhere in the nation, people spoke in hushed tones. But nowhere was the hurt felt more deeply than in Ohio, where William McKinley had been born, raised, and started his political career. In Cleveland, Cincinnati, and Canton, church bells called people to prayer, while on farms and in villages throughout the country, families gathered to pray among themselves. Yes, "the old man" in the White House was one of them and always had been—from the very beginning.

Chapter 2

Ohio School Days

"**L**ucky seven!" called out William McKinley, Sr., as he promptly labeled his new son, born January 29, 1843, in a wooden cottage on the corner of a main street in Niles, Ohio. Four girls and two boys had preceded the latest McKinley arrival, but believing in the age-old superstition that luck surrounded the number seven, the proud father immediately declared the latest arrival would carry his own name, with a "Jr." tacked on. His wife, Nancy Allison McKinley, voiced no objection. She merely undertook the usual mothering duties to which she had become accustomed.

THE EARLY YEARS

Young William spent his earliest years listening to stories about his Scotch ancestors as well as Scripture lessons from the Bible. Although both of his parents had no more than grade school educations, they recognized the importance of learning as much as possible about their own family heritage and deeply held Methodist faith. "Whatever you be," the senior McKinleys preached to their children, "you will be a credit to your family and to your God." Just to make certain the thought was understood and never forgotten, a well-used birch rod stood in the corner, ready to be applied if needed.

William McKinley, Jr., was born on January 29, 1843, above this grocery store in Niles, Ohio. The seventh of nine children, the infant was named for his father, who managed the local iron foundry. (Library of Congress.)

Raised in a family of iron workers, William's father spent 12 hours a day managing a charcoal furnace. Before the discovery of a process that revolutionized the steel-making industry, small charcoal furnaces dotted the country, each producing small amounts of pig iron for local regions. William Sr. chopped trees, split logs into firing lengths, burned wood to make charcoal, and looked for iron ore. It was hard work, demanding long hours and physical strength, but "useful labor, suitable for a strong man and a hearty Christian soul," so the elder McKinley remarked often.

As soon as he was old enough, William McKinley was added to the throng of youngsters attending the one-room schoolhouse in Niles. Books were scarce, making "pure learning even more difficult to acquire," noted the older McKinley. But young William took to reading, writing, and arithmetic quickly. He also got along well with his peers. Out of school, there were the usual games of hide and seek in the surrounding woods, splashing in Mosquito Creek (where he might have drowned once if a young man had not pulled him out in the nick of time), and playing "Soldier! Soldier!" With exciting tales of the Mexican War drifting back to Ohio, boys of Niles sculpted paper military hats and brandished wooden swords as they made charge after charge up hills and across fields. "I'll be Zack Taylor!" William would call out, enjoying the role of America's great general at that time. "Follow me!" he would shout, taking charge, giving orders, and rallying those around him into action. He was an able hand with a bow and arrow as well, could shoot marbles with great accuracy, and even older boys would follow his lead. "He was just like other boys, except that he was of more serious turn of mind," his mother later recalled.

THE EDUCATION OF A PRESIDENT

Recognizing the limitations of the crowded one-room wooden schoolhouse in Niles, the elder McKinleys packed up their family in 1852 and moved some 10 miles south to Poland, Ohio. The white frame house in Poland gave the large family more space, and the local schoolhouse was better equipped than the one in Niles. After young William passed quickly through the studies offered in the local public school, he entered Poland Academy. The three-story structure boasted four instructors and a variety of class offerings, including instrumental music lessons for students who desired them.

At "the College," as Poland Academy was called, William not only gleaned an education from books and discussions of history, literature, and the classics, he also enjoyed the debating society. He acquired an appreciation for a properly turned phrase and the forcefulness of powerful oratory. Young men at the academy became caught up in the arguments for and against slavery, the issue that threatened to rip the country apart. "We are one nation and must remain united," the fiery William asserted as a teenager. "Individual states must be given only those rights that do not threaten the strength of the entire country."

By the fall of 1860, 17-year-old William McKinley had fulfilled the requirements of Poland Academy and headed to Meadville, Pennsylvania, where he enrolled in Allegheny College. His mother made no secret that she wanted her son to pursue the Methodist ministry, but William's mind was still open to future plans. Whatever he chose to do, he pledged to do it well, and he plunged into his studies with determination and dedication. "I study every hour I am not eating, sleeping, or in class," William wrote to the family back home. "I shall attempt to make you proud of my endeavors." Sadly, however, the vigorous schedule took its toll, and William became ill and weak. Reluctantly, he was forced to drop out of Allegheny College and return to Poland to regain his health.

A Matter of Family Honor

Although he had every intention of returning to Allegheny College as soon as he was well enough to do so, William had to change his plans. The death of an uncle put the family deeply into debt because the uncle owed so many bills. Family honor depended upon the clear and honest name of *every* family member, alive or dead, so William joined with his father to pay off his late uncle's debts. Until this was done, no money was available for William's college education.

William immediately began looking for a way to help

pay his late uncle's creditors and to earn money for college. When the position of schoolmaster at a school only three miles from his home became available, William applied for it. Because his reputation as a scholar during his seven years at Poland Academy was well known, he was hired. The job paid $25 a month, and William could have lived with parents of his students. Instead, he chose to walk the three miles to and from school each day in order to help at home with the nine McKinley children.

Teaching proved to be a grueling task, especially since William did not feel well prepared for the profession, and he quickly switched to a job at the Poland post office. Still determined to further his education as soon as possible, William budgeted his funds carefully. The post office chores of selling stamps, sorting mail, and keeping the small working quarters clean hardly tested the energetic young man's talents, but he became recognized as a delightful conversationalist. "Although I clerked in the post office only a short time," McKinley later recalled, "it introduced me to the many different kinds of people that exist in the world. It was a useful phase of my life, that is certain."

WAR

The quiet life that William was enjoying in Poland, Ohio, was soon upset by events that were transpiring elsewhere. The election of Abraham Lincoln to the presidency in 1860 enraged Southern slaveowners, who feared that the new leader would immediately abolish slavery. Eleven slave states withdrew from the Union, forming their own "Confederate States of America." When Confederate guns blasted away at Fort Sumter in the harbor of Charleston, South Carolina, in April 1861, the bloody Civil War began. President Lincoln wasted no time in calling for Union troops to put down this open rebellion.

War fever spread rapidly through the North. The Poland post office attracted many area residents who came in to share their outrage and apprehension over the war. By this time, allegiance for flag and country had been deeply instilled within the young postal clerk, William McKinley, Jr. His desire to join the Union cause was further sparked through heated discussions with a cousin, William Osborne. But with his father again working in iron mines back at Niles, the junior McKinley felt like he was deserting his mother. After all, if he remained at the post office, he could help out with home duties and also help the family financially. Yet emotion sometimes rules, and young William could no longer ignore his desire to join the war effort. A conference with his mother found her unusually understanding. "You must do what is right for you," she observed. "If you decide to fight, we will manage. But you take care, son."

First Battle

Those enlisting from Poland were immediately dispatched to Camp Chase near Columbus, Ohio, where they merged with the 23rd Ohio Infantry Regiment. With eager anticipation, the new Private McKinley donned his blue Union uniform, hoisted his musket, and marched in formation. Most enlistments were only for three-month intervals because most believed the war would soon be over. But William and his cousin signed up for three years, just in case more time would be needed. "I am confident I have made the right decision," William wrote home.

The commander of the 23rd Ohio Regiment was General William S. Rosecrans, who was eager to lead his men into battle. For weeks, the troops did little more than guard roads and bridges in Virginia, at times accidentally killing livestock they thought to be Confederate soldiers. The Union brigade moved around the Virginia countryside, ever ready to face combat. Then, on September 10, 1861, Private McKinley tasted battle for the first time, encountering Confederate soldiers at Carnifez Ferry during a drenching rain. The storm failed to dampen the spirit of the soldiers, however, and McKinley reported that "the effect of victory was of far more consequence to us than the battle itself. It gave us confidence in ourselves and faith in our commander. We learned that we could fight and whip the rebels on their own ground."

But if the battle lifted the spirits of Private McKinley and his cohorts, the following months proved disappointing and depressing. Confined to the boundaries of Camp Ewing, the soldiers fell victim to countless diseases due to poor sanitary conditions and a lack of proper nutrition. These "fevers" among the troops caused more casualties than did any fighting, and McKinley and his fellow soldiers became more disillusioned.

It was April 1862 before the 23rd Ohio Infantry Regiment went into action again, this time at the Confederate-held town of Princeton, West Virginia. Retreating under the Union attack, the Confederates burned the town's buildings. McKinley and his regiment pursued the foe well into the summer, at one time enduring a march of 104 miles in only three days. "The initial glory of war has worn off," William wrote home. "Our days are long and grueling."

By September, the Ohio regiment had joined the forces of General George McClellan. The Union troops led a spirited assault into Maryland, successfully engaging the Confederates in various encounters. But victories were not without cost, as McKinley watched his fellow soldiers fall victim to enemy shells. Recognized for his leadership, William was appointed commissary sergeant, a task which demanded that the maximum number of troops be fed from a minimum of food and supplies. It was no small duty for a young man of only 19.

Up Through the Ranks

On September 17, 1862, one of the bloodiest of all the Civil War battles was fought. That Sunday morning dawned bright and sunny at Antietam, giving little indication of the hours ahead. But shortly after sunrise, the shooting began as Union and Confederate soldiers started fighting with renewed energy. At first, McKinley was safely located two miles behind the front lines, carefully overseeing the dispensing of food to troops as they arrived at the commissary. But when word reached him that those in combat were both weary and hungry, the young sergeant ordered two mule teams hitched to fully stocked wagons. William drove one team himself, enlisting another young recruit to follow his lead. Soon he was in the midst of battle, under fire constantly, but stopping wherever there were hungry and thirsty soldiers. The tasty rations and hot coffee gave the men new strength. Never before had Union troops been fed at the battlefront. At any moment, McKinley could have been killed, torn apart by enemy shells.

The brave commissary sergeant's actions did not go unnoticed. Major Rutherford B. Hayes, one of McKinley's superiors, reported William's valor to military officials, and by the end of the month, William McKinley, Jr., was promoted to second lieutenant. Pleased with the recognition of his efforts, William still felt deep grief over the 200 members of the 23rd Ohio Regiment who were killed or wounded at Antietam.

McKinley saw little more action until the following summer, when Hayes, now a Colonel, led Union soldiers on a pursuit of Confederate raider John Morgan. Morgan was causing constant troubles by leading his band behind Union lines and destroying food and supplies. Finally, Morgan was cut off as McKinley and others swung across southern Ohio and Indiana. Again, Lieutenant McKinley was written up for his courageous actions. He was promoted to first lieutenant of Company E, the corps of hometown Poland volunteers. In addition, he was made an aide to Colonel Hayes.

Other Heroic Deeds

During the spring of 1864, McKinley endured the most trying event of his military career. Assigned to destroy or gain control of Confederate railroads, the Ohio regiment faced not only the assault of enemy soldiers but of weather as well. The earnest young McKinley recorded the trials and tragedy of a troop journey during the bitter March and April of 1864. "It was a rough and trying march over mountains and through deep ravines and dense woods," wrote McKinley, "with snows and rains that would have checked the advance of any but the most determined. Daily we were brought in contact with the enemy. We penetrated a country where guerrillas were abundant and where it was not an unusual thing for our own men to be shot from the underbrush – murdered in cold blood."

Despite such a long and treacherous march, McKinley and the other members of his regiment distinguished themselves in battle when they managed to take Cloyd's Mountain, a strategic position occupied by Confederates. There was to be no rest for the Union brigade, however. Less than two weeks after the victory at Cloyd's Mountain, they were sent to capture Lynchburg, a heavily fortified Confederate stronghold in central Virginia. But this time good fortune was with the southern soldiers, as they forced the Union troops into retreat.

Again and again the Confederates and Union soldiers

skirmished in the Allegheny Mountains and the Shenandoah Valley. When one Union regiment faced capture after being surrounded by the enemy, McKinley volunteered to help. "I think I can lead them out," he told Colonel Hayes. The young lieutenant did exactly that, under a constant barrage of Confederate fire. When the smoke of exploding shells had cleared, there sat McKinley atop his chestnut mare. "It was more than heroism," reported Colonel Hayes. "It was more of a miracle." Impressed, Colonel Hayes recommended his aide's promotion to captain.

News of McKinley's bravery and courage spread among other Union generals, including George Crook and Winfield Hancock. They, too, utilized the services of Captain McKinley, and he won further acclaim at Opequon and Cedar Creek. But slowly, ever so slowly, the war was winding down. Except for short and limited flourishes, the Confederacy was doomed. In April of 1865, the final shots were fired. A weary but noble Confederate leader, General Robert E. Lee, surrendered to the Union military chief, Ulysses S. Grant, at Appomattox, Virginia. The Civil War was over.

Like thousands of others, William McKinley headed home, mustered out of the Union Army with the brevet (honorary) commission of major. Four years before, he had entered the fighting as a schoolboy, filled with glamorous visions of war. Now, at 22, he returned to Poland, Ohio, a changed man. Although he bore no bullet wounds from enemy guns or ravages from diseases, he did carry a hatred of warfare brought on by witnessing friends cut down in battle. The McKinley who left the war was quite different from the one who had entered it. He was also a man seeking direction, searching for a future. The future, however, was uncertain.

Chapter 3

Learning the Law and Politics

Despite his personal opposition to war, William McKinley briefly entertained the thought of making the Army his career. The ugly memories of what he had witnessed during the Civil War weighed heavily on his mind, and he was determined to do whatever he could to avoid any further conflicts that would claim lives and destroy the human spirit.

NEW CAREER

As new industries popped up across the country, signs everywhere called for laborers. Certainly, there were many possibilities from which to choose. The recently discharged McKinley pondered every opportunity. Gradually, he dismissed the thought of a military career from his mind. But he had enjoyed the leadership roles that had stemmed from his four years in the Union Army. His attention now turned to law, with politics, perhaps, to follow later. The legal profession offered a chance to stretch his mental energies, while public service afforded the chance to carry out the wishes of the people.

Law schools of the time were open to anyone wishing to study law and having the funds to pay the bills. Always hard-pressed to cover expenses, the McKinley family was in no position to pay for young William's legal education. However, those who lacked the financial means to attend a law school yet wished to pursue a career in law could obtain a position working with practicing attorneys. Since law schools were relatively new at that time, many people thought that learning from a practicing attorney was a better way of becoming a lawyer anyway. The resourceful McKinley learned of just such an opportunity in Youngstown, Ohio, in the law office of Judge Charles Glidden. Impressed with the eager, young war veteran, Glidden hired William at once. For the next year McKinley clerked in Glidden's office and spent every spare moment poring over law books.

Despite his earnest efforts to learn all he could in Judge Glidden's office, William felt an urge to acquire formal schooling. After consultation with Glidden, McKinley went to Albany, New York, where he enrolled in a law school. He matched his year of independent study in Glidden's office with a year of classroom work, and by the spring of 1867, he felt confident enough to seek admission to the Ohio bar. Another attorney, Frances Hutchins, supported McKinley and he won immediate admission. Because Poland was too small a town in which to begin a legal practice, the new attorney moved to Canton, where his older sister Anna was teaching.

On His Own

Canton, Ohio, was a bustling town, swelling with new settlers and businesses. McKinley fit the busy climate perfectly, making friends quickly and establishing himself in a law office on Market Street. He was slow to make money, however, being too willing to offer free legal advice. When kidded about giving away his talents, the young attorney would only smile at first. He would then reply, "I'd rather have more friends than I could count than money."

One friend, also in the legal profession, proved to be a valuable asset to McKinley's future. George Belden, housed in a law practice in the same building, soon became aware of the constant traffic flow to and from McKinley's office. Suddenly cut down by illness one day and scheduled to take a case to trial the next, Belden called upon McKinley for assistance. "I'd like to help you," William offered, "but I've never tried a case in court before." Belden nodded. "Then it's time you got started." Together, the two men worked for hours. The next day, McKinley not only made an effective presentation, but he won the case. Impressed by the younger man's abilities as well as his willingness to tackle a difficult assignment, Belden offered McKinley a partnership. William eagerly accepted, grateful to work with an experienced attorney.

Guaranteed a steady flow of clients by his association with Belden, McKinley directed his attentions to political activities. He actively spoke on behalf of his former commander, Rutherford B. Hayes, in his campaign for governor of Ohio. Hayes' election to the office delighted McKinley, as did the election of another Civil War leader, Ulysses S. Grant, as President.

Republican Party officials in Canton were quick to recognize McKinley's speaking skills and, in 1869, encouraged him to run for prosecuting attorney of Stark County. The area was a Democratic stronghold, causing the eloquent attorney to have considerable doubt about running for the position. But run he did, and to the surprise of many political leaders, he won.

The Lawyer Takes a Wife

The budding career of William McKinley was noticed by numerous Canton people, including Miss Ida Saxton, recently graduated from an exclusive finishing school in the East and the daughter of the city's leading banker. The good-natured McKinley took a great deal of ribbing from his lawyer friends about his frequent trips to the First National Bank, where Ida worked as a cashier. "Must be putting away quite a hunk of money as often as you visit the bank," his lawyer friends jeered. "Always goes to the same clerk's window, too."

William smiled, never letting the remarks get on his nerves. Soon he was officially courting Ida, and one evening, as they enjoyed a moonlight carriage ride, McKinley proposed. "Surprising enough," McKinley noted later, "the foolish young girl accepted." On January 25, 1871, William McKinley, Jr., took Ida Saxton as his wife in the First Presbyterian Church of Canton. He was 27, she was 23. Banker Saxton generously provided the newlyweds with an impressive two-story frame house on North Market Street as a wedding gift.

The future seemed grand and glowing for the congenial prosecuting attorney from Stark County. Even those who argued cases against McKinley testified to their opponent's honesty and sense of fair play. He pulled no dirty tricks, no underhanded schemes to win a case. Some people called him "Major" out of respect to his past war service, while others used the nickname for the manner in which he commandeered the courtroom.

But despite the respect McKinley had won, the Democrats mustered their forces to win back the office of prosecuting attorney. After a narrow defeat, a disappointed McKinley returned to the practice of law, no longer an officeholder. But the depression he felt was only temporary. On Christmas Day 1871, a special present—a baby girl—arrived at the North Market Street house. The McKinleys named their first child Katherine, quickly shortening it to "Katie."

A GROWING REPUTATION

McKinley's reputation as an attorney was constantly growing, and although he held no elected office, he actively participated in local Republican politics. He was a favorite counsel of young men just getting started in the legal profession, and he would always find time to share his opinions and philosophy.

In 1873, tragedy entered McKinley's personal world. Ida, who was expecting another baby, went into a tremendous prolonged depression after her mother died. The baby, another daughter, was born in March and shared her mother's name of Ida, but was in poor health. Within six months, the baby died, as did four-year-old Katherine two years later. Devastated by the loss of both his daughters, McKinley pledged to devote himself to caring for his wife.

The nomination of his military chief and political ally, Rutherford B. Hayes, for President in 1876, however, cheered McKinley. He volunteered to campaign actively on behalf of his old friend, but Republican officials had more plans than that for the popular Canton attorney. "We'd like you to run for Congress," they told McKinley. Eager to return to the political arena, he accepted. After capturing the party's nomination, McKinley spent the fall of 1876 speaking before any audience who would listen to him. He shied away from any specific political platform and promises, preferring instead to tout his allegiance to Hayes and to guarantee to "work for the people, their needs, wishes, and dreams." In November, when the votes were tallied, McKinley won by an impressive margin of over 3,000 votes. The presidential election, with Samuel Tilden receiving more popular votes than Hayes, ended up in a hotly contested battle in the electoral college. Only after a special electoral commission was formed did Hayes win the presidency, a result that pleased McKinley but cast a shadow over the method of choosing the nation's chief executive.

By the time he was sworn in as a member of the United States House of Representatives, McKinley and his wife had taken up residence at the Ebbit House, a comfortable but not overly plush hotel in Washington, D.C., for government officials and visiting dignitaries. Whatever else might happen, it was essential to McKinley that his wife have every comfort possible. He sensed that the duties of his office would require much of his time and attention, but he was determined that no political office would intrude upon their relationship.

At Work in Congress

Satisfied that his wife was receiving the best care possible, McKinley threw himself into his work. At 34, he was one of the youngest members of Congress, and, as such, he recognized that it was wise to listen carefully to his peers, especially those in leadership positions. "It is clear that one cannot accomplish much by himself," the astute young Canton Congressman wrote home to a lawyer. "Action is only achieved by a team effort—of people working together."

Although the Civil War had ended over a decade before, some wounds had still not healed. Not only were congressmen divided by political parties and philosophies, many could not forget the geographical boundaries of North and South that separated individuals. McKinley soon realized that every effort was needed to avoid alienating those colleagues who still harbored resentments from the bloody and bitter past. Few men were more diplomatic than the House new-

The Election of 1876 —
A Lasting Controversy

In 1876, the year William McKinley made his first bid for national office, the political battles between Democrats and Republicans often turned into verbal slugfests. Candidates hurled charges of crookedness and incompetence at their opponents, while the American voter merely shook his head in dismay and tried to make rational choices.

Leading the Democratic ticket for President was Samuel Jones Tilden of New York, while McKinley's old Army chief and statemate, Rutherford Birchard Hayes, led the Republican ticket. It was a blistering campaign going down to the wire, and even after the popular votes were counted on November 7, the verdict was still in doubt.

The Democratic candidates had triumphed, 4,300,590 votes to the Republicans' 4,036,298, but the election was not over yet. Neither candidate had the necessary 185 electoral votes — Tilden was one shy while Hayes only had 165. Twenty votes were in dispute, open to question. An elector from Oregon was found to be ineligible, while the electoral votes of Florida, Louisiana, and South Carolina were claimed by both Democrats *and* Republicans. Southern Democrats claimed ''carpetbagging'' — the bringing in of northern Republicans to run the political machinery of the three states after the Civil War — and also claimed that vote totals did not reflect the true feelings of the people.

According to the Constitution, the electoral votes would be counted in the presence of both Houses of Congress. Another dispute erupted between the Republican-controlled Senate and the Democratic-controlled House of Representatives. Leaders could not agree on a fair way of counting the votes. Finally, a compromise was reached: a bipartisan electoral commission of seven Democrats and seven Republicans plus one independent, Supreme Court Justice David Davis, was selected to make the official count. Allowing an independent judge to be a part of the process would offer fair resolution to the ongoing struggle for power.

But unexpectedly, Davis retired. Justice Joseph Bradley, a Republican, was named to take his place on the commission. In the midst of much turmoil and controversy, the count began on February 1, 1877, and did not conclude until March 2. Although discussion was heated and prolonged, the end result surprised few people. The commission voted along partisan lines, with eight votes going to Hayes and seven to Tilden. (Most historians feel the Democrats were willing to accept the electoral commission's outcome in return for a promise that northern troops would be withdrawn from the southern states, thus ending the Reconstruction governments and allowing the Democrats a better chance of gaining political control in the South.)

On March 5, 1877, Rutherford B. Hayes took the oath of office as 19th President of the United States. However, because the official inauguration day was March 4, which fell on a Sunday, Hayes was administered the oath privately on Saturday, March 3, so that the government would not be without an elected leader for even one day. But the election of Rutherford B. Hayes continues to endure as the most disputed and controversial in American history.

comer from Canton. His ever-sparkling and penetrating deep blue eyes, brisk walk, and rigid military poise combined with his willingness to listen, compromise, and act won him immediate acceptance by his colleagues in the House. Upon his first encounter with McKinley, Supreme Court Justice John Harlan was said to have remarked to President Hayes, "Keep your eye on that man. He just may be President some day."

For William McKinley, however, his thoughts were not on the presidency. All he wanted to do was to be an able representative. He had been rejected once in the political arena when he was not re-elected prosecuting attorney of Stark County. If he liked this job, he hoped to keep it.

Diving headfirst into his duties, McKinley soon wondered if there was ever an end to the countless committee meetings, correspondence, and visitors to his office. He welcomed those constituents from back home who came in for a brief social exchange or to share an idea or opinion. But too many were looking for some political favor, perhaps a job for a relative or friend. McKinley quickly developed an uncanny ability to sense the motives of such people, and he wasted little time with them. Strangely enough, he could escort them out of his office with the same warmth with which he had welcomed them.

Other politicians did not display as much integrity. They rewarded those who had done favors for them by giving favors in return. It did not take McKinley long to recognize that the government was seriously hampered by this system. He supported civil service reforms, helping to enact laws and restrictions that demanded individuals to be qualified for any governmental position. "The United States government collectively will be only as strong as its individual workers," McKinley asserted. "A job in government is a privilege and a responsibility, never a mere reward for favors rendered."

McKinley was equally firm about the rights of black Americans. Although the Emancipation Proclamation guaranteeing blacks their freedom had been signed in 1863, the machinery of government backing up the document worked very slowly and, in some respects, not at all. "No person should be denied opportunities because of the color of his skin," the Ohio representative declared. "Such a denial undermines the strength of the nation."

But McKinley's support for civil service reforms and civil rights for blacks was not what cast him dramatically into the national spotlight. It was the issue of tariffs that thrust William McKinley into national political prominence.

Chapter 4

"Young Napoleon"

66 **T**he revenue necessary for current expenditures and the obligations of the public debt must be largely derived from duties upon importations, which, so far as possible, should be adjusted to promote the interests of American labor and advance the prosperity of the whole country."

So read the Republican Party platform (their position on national issues) in 1876. In simple words, the Republicans solidly backed a tariff program that would keep out foreign competition. No Republican felt more strongly about that belief than Congressman William McKinley. "It is our duty," he asserted of the high protective tariff, "and we ought to protect as sacredly and assuredly the labor and industry of the United States as we would protect her honor from taint or her territory from invasion."

THE TARIFF ISSUE

McKinley accepted the necessity of high tariffs on imported goods not merely as sound political philosophy and good economics, but as a deep personal cause. Arguments hurled in his direction were met with an icy glare, a reddening of the face, and a verbal outpouring of outrage. And the arguments came often, both before and after his election to Congress.

The Democrats aligned themselves behind a free and open trade policy, charging that tariffs encourage "injustice, inequality, and false pretense." Duties on imported goods were to be applied only to raise money for the federal government, not as a protective device for American industries.

The positions of the two parties on the tariff issue were completely opposite. Ordinarily, the recent national election would have reflected the wishes of the people, and the other side would have backed away. But the election of 1876 was no ordinary one. It was filled with such corruption in voting and counting that the tariff issue still remained highly explosive. President Hayes, recognizing the forcefulness of McKinley's speaking skills and the importance he placed upon maintaining a strong tariff, personally spoke with the Canton representative about the matter. "We need a standard bearer," the chief executive told McKinley, "and you could do the job better than anyone else."

The request was willingly accepted. "I had been told," McKinley shared with a political friend, "that much of politics is having to do things which run contrary to some of your personal ideas and feelings. To be asked by my nation's commander to carry out a mission for which I believe in, heart and soul, is a blessing indeed." Making the position even more palatable was the fact that his own congressional district was continuously sprouting new industries which McKinley felt demanded his personal protection. It was a wonderful way to begin public service, pleasing the hometown crowd while fulfilling national responsibilities.

MAKING AN APPEARANCE

Although the 45th Congress was not scheduled to convene until December of 1877, President Hayes ordered it into session during October. Problems awaited, and it gave McKinley little pleasure to cast a vote overriding Hayes' veto (refusal to approve) in the matter of resuming the coinage of silver dollars. It made him all the more eager to champion a cause both of the men believed in completely.

Although most new members to the House of Representatives waited at least a year before making a formal speech in front of their colleagues, McKinley chose not to wait. He crammed for hours, studying every book, every proposal, anything that had been written about governmental tariffs and finance. There was heavy pressure in Congress to roll back tariffs and allow free trade to pass in and out of the country. "This kind of action is dangerous to the economic stability of this nation," McKinley warned. "Whatever action we take must be deliberate and cautious." Waving a petition from the iron manufacturers in his Canton district, the new legislator called on careful, methodical investigations into the lifting of any tariff policies that might jeopardize American business and industry. Mixing facts and statistics with controlled patriotic emotion, McKinley had Democrats and Republicans alike nodding in agreement. "The boy makes good sense," noted one elderly man to a friend about the 35-year-old McKinley. "Yes, he sure does," came his friend's answer.

A Formidable Sentinel

But despite the respect McKinley gained from his first appearance on the House floor (the Republicans and Democrats voted to accept the newcomer's suggestions), he also made enemies. Clearly he was a coming political force to be reckoned with, and the Democrats hoped to find a way to silence McKinley, but they were unable to do so. If he could not openly prevent tariff changes, he found ways of clogging congressional action by delay and inaction. He sat and stood like a formidable sentinel, dressed in a stylish long-tailed dark coat with trousers to match, high-button black shoes, a stiff white shirt with detachable collar and handsome studs, gold cuff links, and a flat black bow tie. At a hefty five feet seven inches, McKinley looked every bit the sturdy obstacle he was.

Yet the Democrats had the majority in the House of Representatives; therefore, committee leadership positions were given to members of that party, leaving the Republicans without much power. But McKinley wasted little time feeling powerless. "He stands straight and hearty," wrote the editor of the *Canton Repository*, the hometown newspaper. "Whether or not he and his side have a chance of winning a vote, you can be sure that our Representative McKinley will be heard. And when he speaks, it is with preparation and eloquence."

It was a tiring pace at times, and McKinley knew his wife found little pleasure in Washington society. She preferred the calm of Canton, where they could be among family and friends, out of the hectic pace of the nation's capital. Although McKinley realized the responsibilities of his office often prevented him from enjoying his wife's support and company, he found his political tasks totally stimulating and always a challenge. By the time his first term came to an end, he was prepared to mount a re-election bid.

Re-election Time

The Ohio Democrats were making plans of their own. Already McKinley had won more than his share of attention and praise in Washington. The longer he remained there, the less the chance of beating him in the future. "We've got to get rid of McKinley," the political bosses declared. Because of McKinley's public accomplishments and personal popularity, the only way of removing him from office seemed to be by "gerrymandering." (This means redistricting a certain geographical area so that a man in office no longer holds the same base of power.) The process had been introduced in Massachusetts in 1812 by Governor Elbridge Gerry (hence the term), and it had popped up every now and then ever since. In McKinley's case, Democrats controlling the Ohio legislature changed the state's congressional borders so that Republican McKinley was placed in an area where he was far outnumbered by Democrats. His re-election chances were slim indeed.

But slim chances were better than none, and the Canton representative went to work with a determined stubbornness to foil the plans of his adversaries. Wherever a small group of people assembled in the newly constructed district, McKinley gave a speech. He called upon people in their own homes, many of them in heavily Democratic counties that had replaced counties which had more Republicans. "People are people," the campaigner told Ida. "They are willing to listen if you give them a chance."

McKinley's approach was sincere and direct, a salesman selling his customers on the strength of their own country, its stature and potential. He was more than a politician seeking re-election; he was a man with a mission, driven with the ultimate hopes and dreams of guiding a nation into a more perfect tomorrow.

The people listened, and when they voted, they sent Congressman McKinley back to Washington by 1,200 more votes than he had received the first time he had run. "Oh, the good luck of McKinley," exclaimed President Hayes. "He was gerrymandered out and then beat the gerrymander!"

A MORE POWERFUL CONGRESSMAN

With renewed confidence, McKinley returned to Washington. His colleagues in the House knew what he had accomplished in winning the gerrymandered election in Ohio.

Politics—"A Tough Game of Hardball"

"Politics is no game for the thin-skinned or the fainthearted," President Harry S. Truman once remarked. "If you're going to play politics, you've got to expect a tough game of hardball."

William McKinley learned exactly that in the early stages of his political career. First elected to the United States House of Representatives in 1876, he soon made his presence known. He studied hard for every House session, and when he rose to speak, he spoke with fervor and eloquence. Democrats clearly feared the representative from Canton, and when they took over the Ohio legislature, they tried to gerrymander McKinley out of office when he ran for re-election in 1878.

The term "Gerrymander" originated in 1812, when Governor Eldridge Gerry of Massachusetts and his fellow Republicans tried to redistrict the state so as to guarantee political control. The new districts formed weird shapes and patterns. A newspaper editor outlined his own district with a painted line, and the drawing was placed on the wall of his office.

When the famed artist Gilbert Stuart visited the editor's office and saw the sketch, he was fascinated. As the editor explained the meaning of the drawing, Stuart picked up a pencil and applied his own imagination. With a few quick strokes, a head, claws, and wings appeared, causing Stuart to remark,

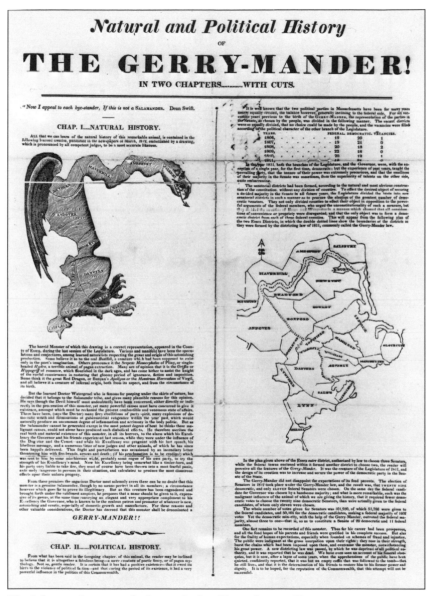

The infamous "gerrymander," named after Massachusetts Governor Eldridge Gerry in 1812, is a devious ploy used by politicians. Voting districts are restructured to swing ballots in favor of certain candidates. More than once, William McKinley was the victim of such tactics. (Library of Congress.)

"Now you have the mythical winged beast called 'the salamander.' "

"Better yet," snickered the equally creative editor, "it could be called 'the Gerrymander' after our noted chief of state."

The story spread quickly, particularly among those opposing the Republican redistricting, and Governor Gerry spent much of his time trying to defend his party's political maneuvering.

Gerrymandering became common in 19th-century politics as individual parties fought to control congressional, state, and city districts. In order to protect rural areas, a number of state constitutions, laws, and statutes were written to provide an anti-urban gerrymander. Because of the shifting and mobility of population, gerrymandering has been especially dangerous in city districting.

McKinley fought off Democratic efforts to gerrymander him out of his congressional position. His opponent in 1878, General Aquila Wiley, thought there was little need to wage an energetic campaign with the new redistricting boundaries. But McKinley, neither thin-skinned nor fainthearted, took to the political field and truimphed, increasing his victory margin by 271 votes over his initial win in 1876.

It was not until 1890 that McKinley was finally defeated as a result of political gerrymandering. Ohio Democrats had carefully carved out a congressional district filled with party members, making it virtually impossible for any Republican to win. That fact, coupled with the feeling against tariffs shared by many Americans and with which McKinley was closely associated, caused him to lose by some 300 votes. But after the loss of his seat in the House of Representatives, William McKinley went on to become governor of Ohio and eventually President of the United States. Thus, gerrymandering may have cost the Republicans a congressman, but it gained them a President. Surely, Harry Truman was right!

William McKinley was regarded with new respect, and with that respect came more power. Before his re-election, he had been merely another member of the Federal Laws Committee, a relatively obscure House group assigned to suggest revisions of national laws as needed. But after the contest of 1878, McKinley's voice gained more listeners, and when efforts were made to promote paper money currency, the Ohio legislator's opinions in favor of hard metal money received added attention.

McKinley also became a stronger advocate of citizen's rights; he wanted blacks to be able to vote. As for Confederate officers returning to the United States Army, he wanted none of it. "Too soon," summed up his sentiments. And as for those whites who wanted to maintain their supremacy in the South, McKinley joined fellow Republican James Garfield in thwarting such attempts. There were many elected officials from the South who wanted a weak federal government with more power given to the states. Because most of these southern officials were Democrats, McKinley gained considerable prestige among his fellow Republicans as he spoke out often and loud against their efforts. "We are the *United* States of America," he often reminded those in the House of Representatives, "not merely the states of America. If we are to be strong individually, we must have a central source of power. That is what we are here for, and we must never forget that honor and responsibility."

Troubles in Ohio

Despite McKinley's ever-increasing stature in the House of Representatives, there always seemed to be troubles back in his native state. By 1880, the Republicans had gained control of the Ohio legislature, and the fear of more gerrymandering was erased. But another problem loomed on the horizon. There were citizens, many in political positions, who felt that two terms were enough for any congressman to serve. From each of the four counties McKinley represented came candidates who wished to challenge him for his seat in the House. Fortunately, however, McKinley was appointed as temporary chairman at the Ohio State Republican Convention, a rather ceremonial job but one which allowed him to speak at the beginning of the conclave. As the keynote speaker, McKinley provided a broad overview of Republican philosophies and goals. His speech was a major success, and for the Ohio Republicans to select someone else to run for his seat in Congress would have been a personal rebuke. So McKinley was chosen to run again.

Once more, an Ohioian—James Garfield—was selected to be the Republican presidential nominee in the election of 1880. McKinley was delighted, since he and the new candidate had shared many causes on the House floor. It was easy campaigning in the home district because McKinley had worked so closely with Hayes, who chose not to seek another term, and with Garfield, who agreed with McKinley on many political issues. The results of the November election found both Garfield and McKinley in the winner's circle.

There was little doubt that Garfield would rely heavily upon McKinley to support much of the administration's key legislation, but tragedy intervened. Six months after Garfield's term began, he was assassinated. Instead of getting the opportunity to promote the policies of his leader and friend, McKinley instead planned the memorial activities in tribute to the fallen chief executive. Because the new President, Chester Arthur, was not as close to McKinley as Garfield had been, the representative from Ohio did not have as much power as he had enjoyed during the Garfield administration.

Lose One, Win One

In 1882, when McKinley again came up for re-election, the Republican organization in Ohio had lost much of its power. Democrats wrestled away many of the congressional seats previously held by Republicans, with McKinley barely squeaking by with an eight-vote win. However, the election results were challenged by McKinley's opponent, Jonathan Wallace, and an election commission decreed that Wallace was indeed the victor.

Discouraged but undaunted, McKinley returned to Canton, where he immediately began to make plans for another try at Congress. Again he used his vibrant speaking talents, charming listeners with his optimistic dreams and hopes for the future. Another politician thrusting a hand inside his coat might have appeared overly dramatic, but with McKinley, it looked perfectly natural, allowing the other hand freedom to wave and emphasize points. "Young Napoleon," he was nicknamed, after the French general, but the labeling did little damage. In November of 1884, McKinley won back his congressional seat by a margin of 2,000 votes.

With the Republicans also winning control of the Ohio statehouse, McKinley found his next two election bids easy and smooth. He was grateful for the comfort, as it allowed him to concentrate on his duties in the House. "Congressman McKinley from Ohio is like a schoolboy cramming for a test," observed fellow House Republican Robert La Follette of Wisconsin, "and he is determined to score the best grades possible. He is always totally informed on every issue, a bank of knowledge about every proposed law. I would hope I might serve my own constituents half as well as Representative McKinley."

THE PROTECTOR OF TARIFFS

Although informed on all measures, it was the tariff that continued to concern McKinley most. Whenever he sensed protective taxes on imported goods were in danger — and Democrats frequently fought for lowering such fees — McKinley was ready to attack. One congressman, Leopold Morse, claimed the high tariff on wool made it impossible for a person to buy a suit for 10 dollars anywhere in the country. The next day, McKinley appeared on the House floor carrying a bulky package. He unwrapped it, revealing a handsome suit — coat, vest, and trousers. With a hand waving high, McKinley announced the attire was purchased for under 10 dollars, "and I have the sales slip to prove it!" Morse, owner of a clothing store himself, could not believe what he saw. He stepped closer, his eyes sparking with disgust. "Under ten dollars! I don't believe it!" Morse sneered. "Just where did you make such a purchase?" McKinley smiled, a spider having lured a butterfly into his web. "Why Congressman Morse, do you not recognize goods from your own store?" The House erupted in laughter and cheers, even McKinley's opponents applauding the presentation they had just witnessed.

But for the most part, maintaining high tariffs on imported goods was serious business with William McKinley, even a sacred responsibility. "Joan of Arc had her Savior, McKinley of Canton has his Tariff," wrote one Ohio newspaper editor. American businessmen and corporate leaders sought McKinley's assistance in establishing new industries. If there was a high enough tax on a product coming into the country, America's entrepreneurs felt safe in producing it. Thanks, for example, to McKinley's efforts to place high fees on imported tin, it became a major national product. Anyone challenging McKinley's tariff policies was accused of undermining the American work ethic, as well as the nation's people and industries.

In 1890, the dynamic legislator from Canton led a House fight to place tariffs on some 4,000 imported goods. (Democrats said there were 10,000 and that McKinley "was trying to strangle all international trade.") The ever-hustling McKinley spent every spare moment shaking hands and making compromises on the House floor. His campaign worked, and the McKinley Tariff Act, after passage by the House and Senate, was signed into law by President Benjamin Harrison on October 1, 1890.

Defeat at the Polls

McKinley had risen to a position of national prominence, but he had problems in his home state. Ohio Democrats were back in power and had again gerrymandered his congressional district, making the election of a Republican virtually impossible. But McKinley was not one to give up without a good fight. Unfortunately for him, however, before election day public opinion turned against the Republicans. Many American manufacturers, feeling safely protected by high tariffs, raised the prices on their commodities. Some companies, having no competition from other countries, enjoyed a total monopoly of their goods in the United States, so they could charge anything they pleased. The increase in prices sent people across the nation into a state of confusion and fear. McKinley's defense of high tariffs sounded hollow indeed in face of what was happening. "Told us he was looking out for us," many folks grumbled, even in McKinley's home district. "Sending us to the poorhouse, that's what he's doing."

There was little McKinley could do. The Republicans were blamed for every price increase, every problem in the nation. No matter how late into the night McKinley campaigned (he turned in 20-hour days meeting voters and giving speeches), the situation was hopeless. "You have done all you could do," observed his staunchest political ally, Mark Hanna. "It's up to the voters now." Wearily, McKinley nodded. He went to Republican state headquarters to watch the results come in. After a brief flurry of strength, his lead dwindled. The final tally found him losing by only 300 votes, certainly a respectable finish considering the gerrymandering that had gone on and the anti-Republican feelings about tariffs.

But defeat it was, and sadly William McKinley headed home, no longer a part of the political world he had grown to love. The future seemed foggy, his next steps uncertain. Yet anyone who knew this man knew he was not a quitter. He would be heard from again. Of that there was little doubt.

Chapter 5

A Man Named Hanna

The name Mark Hanna is not widely known in American history. But in truth, had it not been for Mark Hanna, the name of William McKinley would probably not have been among the list of U.S. Presidents. Rich and shrewd, Mark Hanna played politics cleverly. As a millionaire manufacturer, Hanna had gained wealth and power largely through McKinley's efforts to maintain high national tariffs.

But there was something beyond selfish, personal interests that attracted Hanna to McKinley. The Canton representative had a charisma that Hanna recognized and respected. It was the Ohio Republican State Convention in 1888 that truly solidified the political partnership between the two men.

THE RACE FOR GOVERNOR

As Chairman McKinley banged the gavel and set the tone for the proceedings in Columbus, there was electricity in the air. The delegates had gathered to pick a Republican to be the state's choice for the presidential nomination at the Republican National Convention to be held later. Most assumed John Sherman would be selected, but others looked elsewhere. A few delegates decided that McKinley would be a more promising candidate, largely because of his national prominence due to the tariffs.

But McKinley would not let that happen, or even give it a chance. It would not be honorable. This was John Sherman's time and turn. During the third round of balloting, McKinley stood and announced emphatically that he was *not* a candidate for the presidential nomination. There was no mistaking his tone, no arguing his decision. Clearly, McKinley believed in a code of honor in politics. "He bears watching," Hanna told his associates.

Hanna was watching closely during the election of 1890, when McKinley lost his seat in the House of Representatives. "There's always another election," Hanna told McKinley. "Why, we'll be picking a new governor soon."

If Hanna had hoped to spark McKinley's enthusiasm for the governorship, the thought did not succeed. McKinley saw the governor's position as one of an advisor. It was the legislature that proposed and passed bills. Why, the governor did not even have veto power. McKinley had little appetite for the governor's chair. Not only that, the Democratic incumbent, James Campbell, was well liked and honest. To run against him would be a high-risk gamble. Still smarting from his last defeat at the polls, McKinley saw little chance to stage an upset.

But there was no dissuading the persistent Hanna. Conceding that Campbell was a formidable opponent, Hanna would never admit that he was unbeatable. Few Republicans, perhaps only one, could manage the job. William McKinley was that man.

"I know you are not eager to run," admitted Hanna. "I know your wife has little use for the public spectrum. But sometimes we must look beyond ourselves. If the public wants you, indeed, *needs* you, would you turn from them?"

It was not an easy decision. Ever since the death of their

two children, Ida had become more withdrawn. She had little desire to leave Canton. Yet she would never stand in her husband's way. "Do what you must do," she said often, "and I shall abide by your choice." No, the decision rested squarely with William McKinley himself. To run or not to run—that was the question.

When the Ohio Republicans gathered in Columbus during the summer of 1891, they came ready to do battle. The word was out—McKinley would accept the nomination for the governorship. The race was on!

The Workingman's Friend

And an exciting race it was. Not only did McKinley take on the popular Governor Campbell, the People's Party and the Prohibition Party also fielded candidates. With varying degrees of force and eloquence, those vying for the state's top position traveled all around Ohio, speaking to any group of three or more people who would listen. McKinley defended his stand on high protective tariffs, emphasizing his desire to build strong American businesses and maintain high employment levels. He expressed his own personal dismay at the leaders of industry who had taken advantage of the protective tariffs and boosted prices of their own goods. The people listened—and they believed.

When the voters went to the polls, the People's Party and the Prohibition Party largely took votes away from those Campbell would have received. McKinley managed to win the governor's spot by some 21,000 votes. Although Republicans dominated the state legislature, it was hardly a unified party, and it was hoped McKinley could use his amiable good nature to pull his fellow Republicans together. In his inaugural address as governor on January 11, 1892, the new state chief executive pledged "a wise, economical and honorable administration" to the people of Ohio.

Not a moment was wasted. Although it was the legislature's job to suggest and pass laws, McKinley knew he could initiate ideas and possible reforms. Conscious of inadequate safety regulations in Ohio businesses, he recommended new safety rules to protect industry workers, especially railroad restrictions. "Any person should be able to work within a safe and healthy working environment," McKinley declared. "To provide any less is to deny our citizens a basic right."

Not only did the new Ohio governor promote better working conditions, he also supported laws that allowed workingmen to form trade unions and to strike, if necessary. Even those who earlier had associated McKinley mainly with business owners and industrial leaders recognized his concern for the workers. He solidified that position by backing taxes on major state corporations, a move that eased taxes on individuals and helped to build the state treasury. "Earlier, when we charged McKinley with being a puppet of big business, either we were wrong or he has changed," wrote one newspaper editor. "He appears to understand the very heart and soul of the working man and his family." Whatever his actions, McKinley took the time to explain his reasons. The people had seldom been given such warmth and attention.

Stories about McKinley and his affection for his wife also traveled across the state and beyond. The loving couple occupied hotel rooms directly across from the capitol in Columbus. When he left for work each day, McKinley would look up at Ida, standing at the window, and wave. At three o'clock each afternoon, he would do the same thing from his office window. Ida attended few social functions, preferring the tranquility of the family chambers, where she crocheted countless pairs of bedroom slippers and donated them to worthy causes.

When the Republican National Convention was held, McKinley led the state delegation as chairman. The obvious choice for the presidential nomination was incumbent Benjamin Harrison. But before the voting had ended, McKinley had received 182 votes. It was obvious that his popularity reached beyond the boundaries of Ohio. "Next time for sure," promised Mark Hanna, and McKinley knew his friend had an astute sense for politics. Harrison was defeated by Grover Cleveland, a Democrat, who became the only man to win the presidency two separate times (not in a row). Despite the opposing party's control of the White House, Hanna immediately began setting up "McKinley for President" clubs.

IN A TOUGH SPOT

During his continuous rise in the national political spotlight, McKinley retained a warm image as a loving husband, loyal friend, and caring neighbor. But it was just this image that almost caused his personal and political downfall.

Robert Walker had been McKinley's friend for many years. When Walker's business started to fail, he went to the governor for assistance. McKinley, always ready to help a friend in need, endorsed and backed up Walker's financial notes. However, instead of getting himself out of debt, Walker's entire business empire collapsed. The generosity he had shown a friend suddenly plunged McKinley $130,000 in debt. McKinley decided that he must leave politics and concentrate on making money as a lawyer. With that change and with an inheritance left to his wife, he thought the debts could be erased.

But Mark Hanna had other plans. He would not hear of Ohio's governor suddenly bowing out of the political arena. The "McKinley for President" clubs were quickly picking up supporters, and Hanna already had his eye on the 1896 presidential election for McKinley. Hanna took McKinley's personal debt as his own, rounded up the necessary funds, and paid it off.

Learning of McKinley's private financial difficulties, the Democrats in Ohio tried to use it for their own political advantage. "How can we expect a man who cannot manage his own money matters to oversee the management of an entire state?" charged one editorial. "The sooner Ohio is rid of McKinley, the better we will all be." The criticism stung the sensitive McKinley, not only for himself and Ida, but also for the embarrassment it caused his friend Walker.

Surprisingly, however, the charges made by Ohio Democrats backfired. The people were not shocked and dismayed at their governor's problems with money; in fact, most citizens looked at the situation as being a friend helping a friend and being caught holding the bag—an empty bag at that! Newspaper editors lent their support. "Anyone who knows William McKinley at all realizes he would help anyone in need," wrote one journalist. "Why, he would probably even help a Democrat! That he should endure the slings and arrows of attackers for merely being kind and generous is sad indeed."

Even the humorist, Mark Twain, added his voice to the battle being waged.

> It seems the governor of Ohio, a certain William McKinley, is being paddled behind the woodshed by those Democrats in his state who frown on the fellow for reaching out to a friend. Now, since I seldom have more than a nickel in my pocket, I have never experienced the satisfaction of being a lender. But a borrower I have been often, and I confess that I am grateful for the likes of Governor McKinley in this world. I would advise those so-called gentlemen who have taken the good fellow to task for his generosity to stop wagging their jaws and get about more important business.

NOMINATION STRATEGY

By the fall of 1895, the controversy over the McKinley loan had subsided, and the Ohio governor could now return to administering rather than constantly having to answer personal questions. From a distance he kept abreast of the political maneuvering of his friend and advisor, Mark Hanna, and by winter, Hanna's strategy was taking a more definite form. Under the guise of a vacation trip to the South, Hanna rented a house in Thomasville, Georgia, and put into operation a timetable that would give McKinley the Republican nomination for President in the summer of 1896.

To some, setting up a Republican camp in the midst of southern Democratic turf would appear foolhardy at best, yet Hanna knew exactly what he was doing. True, the Democrats maintained a tight hold on the southern states, but southern Republicans were tested and true. They would bring delegate strength to the convention and, according to Hanna's figuring, would add to the midwestern delegates who had already shown favor toward McKinley at the last convention.

"But we don't really know the man," southern Republicans protested.

"That's no problem," countered Hanna.

Immediately an invitation was extended to McKinley to bring his wife, Ida, to Thomasville for a restful vacation. Because the southern climate promised a welcome escape from the bitter Ohio winter, the couple eagerly accepted. They soon discovered that it was hardly a real vacation, however, for during the three weeks the McKinleys stayed in Thomasville, they did little more than entertain Hanna's invited guests — all of whom happened to be influential Republicans. Political etiquette (manners) did not allow a potential political candidate to openly announce his intentions to seek nomination for a particular office, especially the presidency, but it was hardly a secret that McKinley was interested in being the Republican candidate for President. Thus, the endless parade of convention delegates calling upon the visiting Ohio governor was hardly just social. The constant entertaining frequently tired the fragile Mrs. McKinley, but her husband never seemed to weary of the political discussions.

With increasing frequency, "McKinley for President"

Not everyone respected the wealthy Mark Hanna, who devoted much of his time and money on behalf of his political cohort, William McKinley. Under a picture of Senator Henry Clay, a frequent contender for the presidency but never a winner, who once said, "I would rather be right than be President," Hanna is telling McKinley "It's better to be President than to be right!" (Library of Congress.)

clubs were appearing in both urban and rural areas across the country. Each group appeared to be well financed and organized, the sure sign of the Mark Hanna pattern. "When that convention is held in the summer of 1896, there won't be a soul in this land who hasn't heard of William McKinley and wants him to be our next President," boasted Hanna.

With the Walker loan situation behind him and his personal popularity growing by the day, McKinley actively campaigned for Asa S. Bushnell as Ohio governor during the late fall of 1895. Ohio politics no longer interested Hanna; he was more concerned with higher stakes. His business office in Cleveland was a collection of maps and graphs, with step-by-step charts plotting McKinley's progress. McKinley himself enjoyed constant newspaper attention as he campaigned for Bushnell. Through shrewd manipulation, Hanna managed to get McKinley's face and speeches printed not only in Ohio but in many other states. "What this man says is news everywhere!" Hanna insisted.

Astute newspaper editors recognized McKinley's potential, sensed his personal goals, and accepted the obligation of keeping their readers informed. Bushnell captured the governorship by a wide margin, with McKinley receiving considerable credit for Bushnell's victory. As outgoing state leader, McKinley addressed the Ohio legislature for the last time. "We're not done with you yet!" hollered one political colleague at the end of the speech. "The next time we'll be voting for you for President!" The ever-poised McKinley simply raised his hand to squelch any further outburst, but there was no misunderstanding his cheerful smile and sparkling eyes.

"NO STRINGS ATTACHED"

After McKinley and his wife returned to their home in Canton, Mark Hanna traveled across the country, making political deals with Republican leaders. Some wanted definite positions and promises in return for their backing of McKinley, but Hanna would have no such arrangements. "You had better teach your boy how to play the game," New York's Thomas Platt told Hanna. "If I am promised a Cabinet appointment," bargained Matthew Quay of Pennsylvania, "I can give McKinley my state at the Republican convention." Still the man in Canton stood firm. "I am grateful for any help," McKinley declared, " but there must be no strings attached."

Not only did McKinley refuse to make political promises, he also refused to accept the backing of the American Protective Association. The APA promoted "100 percent Americanism" and worked actively against Catholics and Jews. In addition, they wanted no more immigrants coming into the country. When McKinley refused to have anything to do with the AAP, rumors began circulating that he was a secret agent of the Roman Catholic Church. At first, McKinley denied the charges, but no sooner would one charge be put to rest than another would spring up. Finally, he chose to simply ignore the organization and its criticisms.

McKinley also chose to remain relatively silent about the national issue concerning money and currency. Due to the discovery of huge silver ore deposits in the West, especially among new states entering the Union, the value of the metal had steadily declined. Gold, on the other hand, had become more and more expensive. By law, the United States was required to purchase between two to four million dollars worth of silver each month for conversion into coins. Republicans argued that the overabundance of silver ore greatly reduced the value of the metal and that currency based on gold would be more sensible. By 1890, one ounce of gold was worth 20 ounces of silver. Democrats, led by their spokesman, William Jennings Bryan, affirmed their faith in the silver standard. Personally, although McKinley leaned toward the Republican thinking in favor of gold, he chose to keep his opinions to himself.

In June of 1896, the Republicans held their national convention in St. Louis. There was little question who the presidential choice would be. Thanks to Mark Hanna and his pre-convention organizational planning, William McKinley was nominated on the first ballot. "Our gathering was little more than a pep rally for the man from Ohio," observed another political contender, Theodore Roosevelt of New York. "Everywhere you looked, you saw pictures of McKinley, and banners and posters." New Jersey's Garret Hobart was selected as the vice-presidential candidate.

The following month, the Democrats met in Chicago. In a more heated contest, they selected Bryan to challenge McKinley. It was a clear repudiation of the present President, Grover Cleveland. But Bryan electrified the Democrats with his powerful oratory, a strength Cleveland lacked completely. Attacking the Republicans and their support of a national gold standard, Bryan championed the workingman's cause. "You shall not press down upon the brow of labor this crown of thorns," Bryan thundered at the absent yet ever-listening Republicans. "You shall not crucify mankind upon a cross of gold!"

McKINLEY VERSUS BRYAN

The race was on, the battlelines drawn. But from the very beginning, the difference in campaigning style became apparent. Bryan took to the road, giving speeches in every state, in circus tents, auditoriums, meeting rooms. Where there were people, William Jennings Bryan would go. At 36, he was young, vibrant, always willing to lift his voice for the Democratic cause.

At 53, Republican William McKinley appeared to be almost a paternal figure in comparison to Bryan. Although he was a practiced and polished orator, he knew he lacked the theatrical exuberance of his adversary. McKinley had no desire to pound a podium or leap around a stage. If that was what audiences wanted, that was their choice. It was not McKinley's style. In fact, the man from Canton decided to wage a totally subdued campaign. While Bryan galloped busily across the country, McKinley stayed home and played the perfect host, welcoming anyone in the country who stopped by. Mr. and Mrs. John Smith received the same hospitality that was accorded to political bigwigs, although there were many more of the latter who took advantage of McKinley's warmth and graciousness. "The table is always set for ten," Ida McKinley wrote to a friend that fall of 1896, " and often we must add plates." Although her fragile health did not permit Mrs. McKinley to entertain with the energy and enthusiasm of her husband, she did all she could on his behalf.

Surprisingly, McKinley's quiet, reserved style appealed to people. As the campaigning drew close to election day, Bryan's fiery oratory seemed almost hysterical, while McKinley welcomed crowds who were chanting, "We Want You, McKinley, Yes, We Do!" He carefully explained his ideas, then distributed pamphlets to visitors as they left. His overall manner had a calming effect, one that gave people a comforting feeling.

On November 5, 1896, Americans went to the polls. Special telegraph and telephone lines brought the results to the McKinley home in Canton. When all the results were in, McKinley received 7,108,480 popular votes and 271 electoral votes. His opponent, Bryan, received 6,511,495 popular votes and 176 electoral votes. William McKinley had been elected the 25th President of the United States.

Chapter 6

Into the White House

On March 4, 1897, a nippy spring breeze ruffled the full-length dresses and handsome morning coats of the dignitaries who were gathered on the Capitol's east portico in Washington, D.C. Tall top hats glistened in the sun, mingling with the fancy flowers and birds that made up the creations adorning women's heads. Most of the gentlemen sported full but neatly clipped moustaches. For the swearing-in of William McKinley as the 25th President of the United States, the rich and the powerful were looking their best.

America, too, was in a mood to celebrate. Seated on the east portico was the outgoing chief executive, Grover Cleveland, who had served the nation twice, from 1885 to 1889 and from 1893 until this very moment. He looked tired, worn by years of trying to hold the country together through economic strain and business depression. Satisfied that he had done all he could to mend the nation's woes, Cleveland was glad to be handing the reins of the executive branch of government over to another, even if he happened to be a Republican.

"NO WARS OF CONQUEST"

And in that moment of change, America seemed to take a deep breath, ready to embark on a new journey. Despite the echoes of labor strife and controversy over money and currency, there was a general mood of good feeling that transcended any minor aches and complaints. Most of the vast terrain making up the United States had now been settled by hearty, adventuresome people. Factories and businesses continued to spring up, requiring more workers and bringing new transportation routes across the length and breadth of the country. One by one, states lined up to be welcomed into the ever-growing Union. With an awareness of the country's power and growth, there were many in America who looked beyond the boundaries of the nation, eager to find lands and people ready for acquisition, to exchange isolationism for imperialism.

As always, William McKinley sensed the feeling of the people. Whether it was an inborn gift or an acquired ability, he understood the thoughts of those who worked in factory and field, who raised the children, who enjoyed the resources of their country and the friendship of their neighbors. He, too, had lived the dream that was America. He had watched it grow and prosper, becoming a powerful giant among the world's nations.

However, McKinley sensed a danger in the country's desire to expand and grow. Would American citizens feel *too* powerful, wanting to reach out and sieze territories and people who might not wish to become part of the United States? This was known as "imperialism," and had happened before in other parts of the world. Such greed, such desire for acquisition, had weakened and even destroyed nations and empires.

As William McKinley took to the podium to give his inaugural address, he carried with him the knowledge of an ugly situation that was occurring in Cuba. The American consul, General Fitzhugh Lee, had conspired with others to separate the island from its mother country, Spain. He knew Congress and most Americans would welcome an opportunity to flex the country's military muscle and simply acquire

Cuba by force. Right or wrong, it could be done. But if it was not right legally, morally, or in any other way, McKinley would have none of it.

"We want no wars of conquest," the newly installed President declared to the audience. "We must avoid the temptation of territorial aggression. War should never be entered upon until every agency of peace has failed." Nancy Allison McKinley, 88 years old and destined not to live out the year, nodded at her son's words. And one foot away, Ida McKinley looked intently at the man with whom she had shared most of her life, buried two children, and met thousands of people. Grover Cleveland mulled over his successor's thoughts, hoping that McKinley's peaceful dream could be achieved.

McKinley continued speaking of other areas of national concern. He supported the continuation of civil service reform and an equitable control of trusts. The Merchant Marine needed to be restored, he said, and careful attention given to the needs of America's workingman. He affirmed his faith in the family unit, thanking his own for their love and support.

RUNNING THE COUNTRY

After a day of parades and celebration, McKinley directed his attention to the running of a nation. It soon became clear that a man assuming the presidency did not start his term with a clean desk. Leftover items remained from the Cleveland administration; problems demanded immediate and wise decision making.

Civil service reforms that had been instituted during the past 20 years authorized the hiring of government employees based solely on ability and experience. Nonetheless, there were many Republican political leaders who expected patronage rewards for having helped in McKinley's election. McKinley would have none of this, issuing statements that no person was to be employed unless "totally qualified for the job assigned."

Although the Senate and the House of Representatives boasted substantial Republican majorities, there was little evidence that both legislative chambers would automatically give their support to the Republican President. On the contrary, many elected Republican officials sided with Democratic policies and thinking, especially in the controversy over silver and gold standards. McKinley knew it would take all of his personal magnetism and public support to pressure Congress into backing his programs.

Foreign Affairs

But if problems within the nation were big, problems beyond the country's boundaries were gigantic. McKinley realized there were many people in the United States, some in positions of power, who had little patience in dealing with smaller nations. The mood of the moment was to settle international disputes quickly, always with a firm American hand that would prevent future occurrences. But McKinley was a man with a conscience, wanting to do the bidding of the people, yet ever aware of what was right and fair.

There was trouble with Canada concerning the Bering Sea fisheries that bothered McKinley in many ways. Greedy seal hunters were killing the creatures at a rate that was rapidly decreasing the size of the herds. It was a matter that McKinley felt deeply about but was frustrating to handle.

Because Canada was under British dominion, the problem could not be resolved directly by negotiations between Washington and Ottawa; everything had to go through London. Despite American efforts to settle the matter quickly, communications with London were complicated and taxing. The entire situation proved totally annoying to McKinley.

American interests in Samoa were equally bothersome. For over two decades, the United States had promoted commercial development and territorial expansion in the southern Pacific. When Germany also indicated a desire to acquire colonial territory in that area of the Pacific, tension mounted. Warfare between the United States and Germany was prevented only through the fateful intervention of a murderous typhoon that destroyed the military capability of both sides. Thereafter, the two countries joined with England to form a three-way protectorate over Samoa, but there was constant tension among the trio of governing bodies.

Japan and Hawaii

The Hawaiian Islands also threatened to become a source of international dispute. For many years Americans had poured money into businesses and farms on the islands, and the United States government had a naval base at Pearl Harbor. In 1893, with the help of the American consul in Honolulu, a revolution was staged to wrest the islands away from the rule of Queen Liliuokalani and annex them to the United States. When he learned of the conspiracy and the complicity of U.S. government officials, President Cleveland refused to promote Hawaii's annexation. "We shall welcome any territory who would come to us willingly," he declared, "but we shall not be a party of this kind of underhanded maneuvering." Recognizing Cleveland's viewpoint, McKinley nonetheless encouraged acquisition of the Hawaiian Islands, if annexation was still desired by the Hawaiians.

But the plan soon ran into trouble. Following Cleveland's reluctance to push for American annexation of the Hawaiian Islands, the Japanese government started to increase its interest and power in the area. The number of Japanese-held islands in the Pacific was increasing rapidly, and the Hawaiian Islands seemed a natural outlet for the expansion of Japanese business and trade.

But Hawaiian officials wanted to stop the dramatic inflow of Japanese immigrants. Once a new executive took over the presidency of the United States, they hoped that perhaps annexation plans might be revived. Only weeks after McKinley was sworn in, Hawaiian leaders ordered a drastic reduction in the number of Japanese entering the islands. Hundreds arrived only to be turned around and sent home. Enraged, Japanese government officials sent a fully equipped warship to sit in Pearl Harbor.

Undaunted by the Japanese show of force, American officials drew up and signed a treaty of annexation with Hawaiian leaders. Three American warships were immediately dispatched to Pearl Harbor. McKinley felt uneasy about the action, feeling that clouds of war were forming. He was even more reluctant to grant the request of a minister, Harold Sewall, who wanted the United States to land a military force on the islands in order to show the Japanese America's commitment to the area. McKinley's hesitancy was backed up by the State Department, but Sewall insisted that a show of American muscle was imperative. "We are treading on dangerous waters," McKinley warned. Sewall was convinced he was right. "The action we take in Hawaii will send a message to the world," the minister retorted. "We cannot appear to be threatened or intimidated. Let us land our soldiers so that Japan and everyone else can see our strength. We will not need to spend one bullet."

Sewall's advice proved correct. By the time the Hawaiian Islands were peacefully annexed by a joint congressional resolution in July of 1898, Japanese officials merely mumbled their disappointment and dismay.

But the problem with Spain over Cuba was not to be as easily remedied. For William McKinley, this would prove his greatest test as President of the United States.

Chapter 7

War!

Located only 90 miles from the southern tip of Florida, the island of Cuba had existed in a general state of harmony and peace under Spanish control since the days of Christopher Columbus. American businessmen had invested considerable money in the island's land and commercial enterprises, drawing a healthy return of profits. But in the waning months of the Cleveland administration, rumblings of revolution were heard, led by Cuban rebels wanting to shake off Spanish domination. Not wanting any American involvement in the matter, President Cleveland managed to skirt definitive action by the United States. He hoped the situation would simply resolve itself on its own.

CUBA LIBRE

But that was not about to happen. By the time McKinley entered the White House, the sparks of Cuban revolution had been fanned into a flame. In May of 1897, McKinley requested that Congress appropriate $50,000 for the relief of Americans in Cuba. The Americans were encouraged to return to the United States until all hostile action in Cuba had ended. Some took that advice, while those who stayed supported the Cuban people. "We had to fight the British to win our freedom," the Americans who remained behind declared, "and you must fight off the Spaniards. It is worth the fight!"

63

The Cuban rebels, called *insurrectos*, needed little encouragement. Armed with machetes and old rifles, they waged frequent and surprise attacks on Spanish military outposts. *Cuba Libre!* ("Free Cuba!") was their battle cry, as they burned Spanish supply buildings, destroyed strategic railway depots, and burned sugar plantations belonging to Spanish landlords. Frustrated and furious, Spanish soldiers swooped down on villages and towns, made mass arrests, and subjected the Cuban rebels to hideous torture. Greatly disturbed by news dispatches, McKinley still hoped to keep the United States out of the turmoil.

But as McKinley attempted to avoid any military intervention, two powerful journalists exploited the Cuban/Spanish crisis to boost sales for their competing newspapers. Joseph Pulitzer, owner of the *New York World*, and William Randolph Hearst, owner of the rival *New York Journal*, sensed an opportunity to capitalize (make money) on the bloody rebellion taking place in Cuba. Reporters from both newspapers were sent to the island with explicit orders to send back the most sensational stories that they could find. "And if you can't find any," Hearst challenged, "make a few up." Newsmen from both papers followed their leaders' directives, and soon Americans were reading endless accounts of the rebels' noble fight, the tortures inflicted by the heartless Spaniards, the senseless destruction of homes and businesses. Each of the newspapers carried a cartoon labeled "The Yellow Kid," and the flashy and often distorted reporting was given the nickname "yellow journalism."

THE SINKING OF THE *MAINE*

Many Americans were deeply moved by the courage and spirit of the Cuban *insurrectos*, causing some political leaders in the United States to cry out for help on their behalf. In addition, there was a renewed urge to expand the United States beyond its existing borders and acquire smaller nations under siege or in need. McKinley, however, continued to urge a peaceful settlement of the Cuban crisis.

February 1898 proved to be a fateful month in the Cuban/Spanish conflict. On February 9, the *New York World* printed a letter sent by Dupuy de Lôme, the Spanish minister in Washington, to a friend. Never thinking his communication might be made public, the minister heaped scorn upon McKinley in the letter. He wrote that "McKinley is weak and a bidder for the admiration of the crowd, besides being a would-be politician who tries to leave a door open behind himself while keeping on good terms with the jingoes (expansionists) of his party." The insults hurt, and aides close to the President noted that he retired early for the night upon learning of the communication. Despite the personal abuse, McKinley still remained firm in his efforts to avert American involvement in the conflict.

However, less than a week later, on February 15, the United States battleship *Maine* exploded and sank in Havana harbor. The disaster killed 266 men—most of the crew—and an American commission was immediately sent to investigate the cause of the explosion. Front-page headlines in the *World* and *Journal* placed the responsibility directly on Spain, and editorials demanded that war be declared. Across the country, other newspapers picked up the demand. "Remember the *Maine!*" headlines blasted, "To hell with Spain!"

Troublesome Government Officials

McKinley still adamantly refused to be caught up in the war fever sweeping the country. Often he recalled the sights and sounds of the fighting during the Civil War, when he had personally witnessed bodies being torn apart and heard the screams of dying men. "Too soon we forget," McKinley told his aides. "After a certain length of time, war takes on a romantic image, and suggests excitement and adventure. Can we

After the American battleship Maine exploded in Havana harbor on February 15, 1898, it was only a matter of time before the United States went to war against Spain. But even though hostilities had ended by the end of the year, McKinley bemoaned the thought that he would be recorded as a "wartime President." (Library of Congress.)

not remember that war is death and destruction? It is a hollow victory that is won at the expense of lost men and broken families."

An effective secretary of state might have been able to steer the country away from the course of confrontation on which it was heading. Sadly, however, McKinley's choice for secretary of state, John Sherman, seemed much more able to cause problems than solve them. At 74, Sherman had clearly become senile and unable to function effectively in the complicated world of international affairs. Even while a treaty of annexation was being drawn up for Hawaii, Sherman told Japanese officials no such action was even contemplated. When the treaty was announced, it caused Japan to distrust America. Compounding the difficulty, Sherman gave an interview to reporters from the *New York World*, labeling Japan as "dangerous" and England as being "more bluff than anything else." He also forecast that Spain would lose in their efforts to keep Cuba, despite McKinley's obvious and repeated attempts to maintain objective neutrality.

General Fitzhugh Lee, the American consul in Havana, also caused McKinley much trouble as he tried to maintain peace. Lee clearly supported the Cuban rebels, even to the point of offering sanctuary to some of them as they were being pursued by Spanish soldiers. Unfortunately, Lee's actions were observed by Spanish officials, causing Spanish leaders back in Madrid to think that McKinley was saying one thing publicly while privately directing American representatives to assist in the revolution.

Spreading War Fever

For five weeks a naval commission investigated the cause of the *Maine* explosion. In the meantime, war fever continued to spread in the United States, fanned by the inflammatory stories appearing in the press. Republican leader Theodore

Roosevelt raised his voice to demand increased naval appropriations to build more ships, and Congress appropriated $50 million. Plans for a canal through the Isthmus of Panama took a big step forward as congressmen recognized the importance of having a major military presence in that region.

Although President McKinley tried to be peaceful and patient, always hoping for some magical cure that would successfully heal the differences between the Cuban rebels and Spain, it just did not happen. More and more pressure came from influential Americans demanding some action. Finally, McKinley gave in. He dispatched a note to the Spanish government in Madrid calling for an end to the bloodshed and fighting in Cuba, regardless of terms. Convinced that McKinley was now aligned with the *insurrectos*, the Spanish leaders refused to accept the American demands for settlement.

On March 20, results of the *Maine* investigation were made public. The tragic explosion was determined to have been caused by a naval mine, planted by unknown parties. Despite the lack of proof, the yellow journalists pointed their accusing fingers at the Spanish, claiming that whether or not the mines had been placed to destroy rebel or American vessels, the damage that resulted could not be undone. Once more, the call for revenge was heard across the country— "Remember the *Maine!*" (Strangely enough, a Spanish commission investigating the *Maine* explosion determined that some internal device had exploded, suggesting that the mishap might have occurred due to an accident. But few people had any interest in such conclusions, as the climate for war was everywhere.)

In addition to the problems with Spain, McKinley was also deeply troubled over the health of his wife, Ida. Her epileptic seizures were occurring more frequently, often during afternoon or evening social events. Trying to minimize the awkwardness felt by guests, McKinley simply placed a

William McKinley's devotion to his beloved wife, Ida, was legendary. Although her health did not allow her to function actively as a White House First Lady, she was admired by Americans across the nation for her willing support and concern for her husband. (Library of Congress.)

white handkerchief over his wife's face. In a matter of minutes, she revived, seemingly unaware that anything had happened.

Diplomatic Efforts

McKinley went before Congress to explain the results of the naval inquiry into the *Maine* disaster. As always, he understood the mood of the people, the majority of whom felt that war was inevitable. Nonetheless, McKinley hoped that a diplomatic conference in Havana might still bring about a peaceful settlement. If only Spain would grant Cuba independence, perhaps war might be averted. Special arrangements were made to install a telegraph between Havana and Washington so that the President could learn the results of the conference immediately. Unfortunately, Spain was only willing to make a few reforms in Cuba; there would be no independence.

McKinley prepared a message to be delivered to Congress on April 6, but before it could be presented, he received an unusual request. A group of European countries and the Vatican wanted to enter the negotiations for peace. It was evident that the Spaniards would have little chance of winning any military conflict with the United States. Once Spain lost Cuba, there would be little to stop the United States from looking around for other possible acquisitions. It was no secret that there were many in the country who relished the thought of adding to the list of U.S.-controlled territories. But despite the intervention of the European delegation, Spain would only agree to a cease-fire, which was not enough to appease the voices in Congress calling for immediate action.

Since taking office, McKinley had enjoyed a good working relationship with Congress. But its members had little use for his recommendation of "neutral intervention"–action calling for Spain to make concessions to the rebels of Cuba. One senator proposed an amendment officially recognizing the new revolutionary government of Cuba. McKinley protested the action, arguing that the U.S. Constitution gave to the President, not Congress, the right to recognize foreign governments. The amendment fizzled and died, but the wheels of war were already rolling.

WAR BEGINS

On April 20 McKinley signed papers calling for active U.S. intervention in Cuba in order to stabilize the government and bring security to the people. Spain completely rejected America's right to take such action, calling it "a clear interference in matters outside their jurisdiction." Diplomatic relations crumbled, and on April 25, 1898, the United States officially declared war on Spain.

One of the first actions taken by President McKinley was to ask for the resignation of Secretary of State Sherman. Since his appointment, Sherman had continuously caused the nation one embarrassment after another, largely through lapses of memory. With the country at war, there could be no chances of possible diplomatic mishaps. Sherman was replaced by a State Department assistant, William R. Day. At the same time, a blockade of Cuba was set into motion, and Commodore George Dewey, commander of the U.S. Navy fleet in the Pacific stationed in Hong Kong was ordered to attack the Spanish fleet at Manila, in the Philippine Islands.

Fighting in Cuba

If the United States had readied itself for war in spirit, it was hardly prepared in any other way. "We can take them!" boasted those men in Congress who had for months been calling for military action. But in truth, from the moment war was officially declared, the United States was in no position to wage any kind of a major offensive. Land troops, limited by Congress to 25,000 soldiers, were needed in both Cuba and the Philippines. Time was also needed to recruit and train new men. Moreover, guns, ammunition, and supplies were needed, too. But the United States had one major advantage on its side—Spain was even less prepared and even more inept in the handling of its military activity.

In June 1898, a force of some 17,000 American soldiers went to Cuba. They joined the fleet of American ships in Santiago harbor, eagerly climbing aboard the vessels from gunboats and makeshift rafts. Then, just as Dewey had demolished the Spanish fleet in the Philippines, the United States scored a similar success in Santiago Bay. But as one ship's captain observed, "It was hardly a victory of which we could be proud. They were simply worse than we were."

Once on Cuban soil, American soldiers found their deadliest enemies were not the Spaniards, but malaria and yellow fever. Of the 5,462 soldiers who lost their lives in the Spanish-American War, only 379 died in battle. The rest of the deaths were caused by malaria and yellow fever.

SPAIN SEEKS PEACE

Recognizing the eventual outcome of the conflict, the Spanish requested that neutral French negotiators initiate peace discussions in July. Once terms for the discussions were agreed upon, a final peace conference was scheduled for Paris in the autumn. McKinley sighed with relief. And when one senator expressed some disappointment that the war was ending before it had barely started, the President remarked, "I was not aware that *you* had volunteered to fight, sir."

Final negotiations called for Spain to relinquish Puerto Rico and Guam to the United States as a payment for having to engage in open warfare. In addition, the Philippine Islands were purchased for $20 million from Spain.

Although the fighting in the Spanish-American War lasted only four months, no one suggested to the man in the White House that the conflict was too short. To William McKinley, no war was ever too short.

Chapter 8

An Age of Imperialism

The facts and figures of the Spanish-American War were short and simple. On April 25, 1898, the United States officially declared war against Spain. On May 1, Commodore Dewey scored a naval triumph over the Spanish fleet in Manila Bay. On May 10, American soldiers landed in force at Guantanamo Bay in Cuba. The Spanish fleet at Santiago Bay was destroyed by U.S. ships on July 3. American troops landed in Puerto Rico on July 25, meeting little resistance. By August 15, the war ended with the unconditional surrender of the Philippines. The conflict had cost the United States some $250 million.

AN EXPANDING COUNTRY

When President McKinley delivered a second report to Congress about the Cuban problems in December of 1898, it was a far different account from the one of a year before. Only 12 months previously, he had shared with Congress his concerns about the escalating difficulties in Cuba. Now the American flag was snapping in the breeze not only over Cuba, but over Puerto Rico and the Philippine Islands as well. Barely noticed during the summer was the official annexation of the

Hawaiian Islands on July 7, 1898, which took place in the midst of the Spanish-American fighting. Those who favored U.S. territorial expansion must surely have been pleased with these events. The chains of American isolationism had been broken; U.S. boundaries had been greatly expanded.

But while this realization brought pride to many who strongly supported a wider role for the United States in world affairs, there was little joy felt by the man who occupied the White House. He lived with an awareness that he would now be numbered among the "war Presidents." For the kind and gentle McKinley who had gone to war and learned quickly to hate it, it was a specter that would haunt him for the rest of his life. "No one ever really wins a war," he wrote. "War, in every sense of the word, is a defeat."

RETURNING TO NORMAL

Always conscious of the needs of the nation, President McKinley attempted to return to his normal pre-war schedule. He began each day with the mail, personally answering as much of it as possible. Visitors were always welcome, with or without appointments. Many politicians came with requests for favors, and McKinley was willing to listen and weigh the pros and cons of every request. His warmth and hospitality seemed able to win over even those with raging tempers. "I went into the man's office planning to skin him alive," observed one senator, "and by the time I left, I was complimenting him on his choice of ties. He does know how to handle folks, I would say."

Cabinet sessions were held on Tuesdays and Fridays. McKinley would listen keenly to the dullest recitation of facts and figures, only to snap back a clear summary of the report presented or to ask key questions. "A President cannot know everything that is going on in a government as complicated as this one," he noted, "but it's his job to listen closely to those who should."

"The Gilded Age"

The business of the nation moved along rather smoothly. A general enjoyment of life was experienced by a large part of the population, leading the world's foremost humorist, Mark Twain, to call the period "The Gilded Age." In addition, new businesses and industries were being established in recently explored territories, attracting workers and their families. McKinley also continued to maintain that gold should be the standard on which U.S. currency should be based. William Jennings Bryan's warning that American interests would be hung "on a cross of gold" was now but a distant memory. McKinley was the one the people heard, and in 1900, Congress passed the Gold Standard Act.

As President of the United States, William McKinley occupied a symbolic position as head of the Republican Party. But often he found himself at odds with fellow Republicans. McKinley still smarted from the verbal insults cast at him during the Spanish-American War. Some of the most vicious barbs had come from a political peer, Theodore Roosevelt, who had been serving as an assistant secretary of the U.S. Navy. Eager to take on the Spaniards and disgusted with McKinley's hesitancy, the swashbuckling Roosevelt declared that McKinley "has no more backbone than a chocolate eclair." Veteran politician that he was, McKinley allowed such taunts to go unchallenged, but he could neither forgive nor forget.

McKinley was also very much aware of those who wanted the United States to acquire whatever lands and territories it could. Most of these would-be "imperialists" were Republicans, wanting to build an American empire. Democrats and Populists made up the anti-imperialists, people who favored strengthening the United States within the limits of its boundaries and conscious that the assimilation of foreign people and cultures was never an easy process.

In many ways, McKinley found himself in the camp of

America's Beloved "Scoundrel"

As the 19th century came to an end, Americans found themselves debating many positions, including how the nation should occupy its place in international affairs, whether currency should be based on gold or silver, and just how many rights a woman should have in society.

But there was little argument as to who reigned as America's greatest writer. Even President William McKinley, who seldom gave personal opinions beyond the political spectrum, could not hold back his admiration for the man born Samuel Langhorne Clemens. "Our country boasts the greatest and grandest of resources," observed McKinley, "not the least being Mark Twain."

Clemens was born in 1835, the same year that Halley's Comet reappeared in the heavens. Growing up in the nation's heartland, Clemens traveled up and down the Mississippi, storing up memories that would spill out onto paper and win him millions of reading fans. He loved riverboats; some 1,000 of the vessels docked yearly in Clemens' hometown of Hannibal, Missouri. When he launched his professional writing career, his choice of "Mark Twain" as a pen name seemed only natural. "Mark Twain" is the nautical term used by riverboat captains for the measurement of two fathoms (12 feet) of water.

A local newspaper, *The Missouri Courier,* provided the ambitious Twain with the opportunity to acquire basic printing and writing skills. But he soon longed to see more of the world, experience life beyond Missouri borders, and taste the treats of new horizons. But in another sense, Twain never left Hannibal, for he constantly reached back in his stories and essays to recapture the characters and events of his youth.

Not only did he prove himself the master of humor and satire on paper, Twain found an appreciative audience for his lectures as well. *Tom Sawyer, Huckleberry Finn, Innocents Abroad* and so many other favorites came to life as their author hopped across the nation like his own "Celebrated Jumping Frog of Calaveras County," leaving people laughing at themselves in theaters and arenas. It was during such a trip that the humorist met, fell in love with, and married Olivia Langdon of Elmira, New York. Their three daughters, Susy, Clara, and Jean, provided a special joy to Twain's life.

The secret of Twain's writing success lay in his ability to recreate the past with exciting yet sensitive nostalgia, as well as capture the present with poignant accuracy. Yes, Americans could laugh at themselves as they read and listened to the humorist's observations, but there was also a possibility these same people might try to improve their own behavior. Twain labeled the final years of the 19th century as "The Gilded Age," reflecting his feeling that although times might appear to be good, perhaps it was a surface appearance, destined to change.

As he approached his own sunset years, Twain observed, "Life has been good to me, better than it should have been. Somehow I have managed to hide the true scoundrel that dwells within me." Twain had predicted he would exit the world as he had entered — with Halley's Comet. In 1910, he did exactly that. As the celestial body disappeared in the night sky, the dazzling star of American literature also departed, leaving behind a collection of masterpieces that still delight young and old readers alike.

the adversary. After all, he had achieved national prominence by waging an active campaign to protect American economic interests through a high protective tariff. "I was elected to govern the United States of America," the weary McKinley confided in his mentor, Mark Hanna, who had become a senator. "Now I am to govern people whose language I neither speak nor understand. Should we not do all we can to make our own nation strong before reaching out to others?"

Continuing Troubles

If U.S. leaders thought there would be no more problems with Cuba and the Philippines, they were greatly mistaken. General Emilio Aguinaldo had nobly championed the Philippine insurrectionists against the Spaniards, assisting greatly the American cause. Not feeling adequately rewarded for his actions, Aguinaldo organized his own troops and led attacks against U.S. soldiers who had remained on the island of Luzon after the Spanish-American War had ended. Neither side was well supplied with arms and ammunition, and the warfare was slipshod and poorly planned. Nevertheless, Ameri-

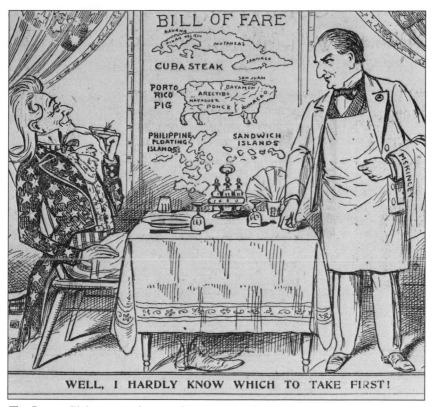

The Boston Globe *was only one of many national newspapers to call attention to America's growing imperialistic attitudes. In this cartoon, published in May 1898, President William McKinley portrays an eager waiter for the country's orders.*

can soldiers were being killed, so the U.S. government quickly sent fresh troops and supplies to the battle areas. It was a long, drawn-out conflict—a constant irritation to McKinley, who detested the continual association of his administration with war. "No President could have hated war more than I do," McKinley mused aloud to his aides, "and yet it would seem no President has been plagued with so many military encounters. Is there an inborn nature within man, at least some men, that comes alive once he attains power and forces him to forcefully engage others in combat? It would seem so."

With meager troops and supplies, Aguinaldo had little

American troops in the Philippines had to continue fighting against the soldiers of Philippine General Emilio Aguinaldo after the end of the Spanish-American War. Here, a wounded Philippine insurgent who has been captured awaits transportation to an American hospital. (Library of Congress.)

chance against the Americans. He managed to wage some form of organized resistance until 1899 and was finally captured two years later. In June of 1901, McKinley supervised the establishment of a peaceful government in the Philippines. Future President William Howard Taft became the official colonial governor of the islands in 1901, but the Philippines had to wait until after the end of World War II, in 1946, to receive final independence.

PROBLEMS AT THE WHITE HOUSE

As if the major and minor conflicts beyond U.S. boundaries were not enough, McKinley encountered hostilities of a different kind within his own home—the White House. Other Presidents might have been able to ignore the situation completely, but the ever-amiable McKinley, always conscious of his wife's health and determined to shield her from all day-to-day worries, found himself annoyed by the complicated social structure associated with the roles they occupied.

Ordinarily, the First Lady directs all entertaining that goes on at the White House, allowing her husband to concentrate on matters of state. But because of Mrs. McKinley's frail health, there was no one to carry out those duties officially, yet there were many willing to usurp those responsibilities and function in her place. In the absence of Mrs. McKinley, administration wives jockeyed to assume leadership roles, guiding the way in fashions and manners.

No one, however, could assume the roles occupied by two top aides, Captain Theodore Bingham and Addison Porter, who decided that they—and they alone—should determine what people should wear to White House functions, who would be invited to which parties, and where guests should be seated in relationship to the President at formal state dinners. At first, McKinley paid little attention to such matters, but as time went on and invitations demanded specific attire, he began to take notice. Matters were further complicated when American naval leaders, including Commodore Dewey, returned as heroes of the Spanish-American conflict and felt themselves considerably above Army generals in stature at official gatherings.

Although Mrs. McKinley could not actively function as White House hostess, she nonetheless was aware of the bickering that was going on, and it distressed her greatly. "Put your mind at rest," McKinley told her, "for I'll not be losing a moment's sleep over such things."

But in truth, the situation did indeed bother the chief executive, as he was the kind of man who did not want to see anyone's feelings hurt. Finally, after reading an article in the *Washington Evening Star* which stated that ladies visiting the White House were not to wear bonnets, McKinley exploded. "Who is making such decisions?" he thundered. "Why, these pronouncements sound like the Ten Commandments of God! No bonnets indeed! I am a bit more interested in what people are carrying inside their hats rather than the hats themselves!" McKinley then wrote a nasty (for him, it was nasty, but for others, it was mild) letter to the *Evening Star.* But the staff members who had made the rules felt they would be humiliated by McKinley's rebuttal and persuaded him not to send his letter. The White House atmosphere warmed considerably after that, and the former strict rules disappeared.

A Murder in the Family

The controversy raised over White House dress codes and social rankings was a small matter compared to the events of October 1898. The family of Ida Saxton McKinley had always prided itself on being pillars of the Presbyterian Church in Canton, as well as leaders of the banking community in the area. Ida's parents, James and Catherine Dewalt Saxton, saw that their son and daughters received the quality of education due the wealthy and refined, with trips to Europe as an appropriate climax to the years of formal learning. Neither parent lived to see the scandal that shook the McKinley and Saxton families and put Washington society into a tailspin.

George Saxton, Ida's only brother, had never managed to live up to family hopes and expectations. Handsome in appearance and quick with words, he took little note of family business but preferred instead to win the hearts and attentions of as many ladies as he could. One such conquest, a married woman who could not stand the hurt of George's eventual farewell, took a pistol in hand and shot him to death. The Hearst and Pulitzer newspaper reporters, experienced in the art of sensationalism from the still-smoldering embers of the Spanish-American conflict, took to the scandal with ripe appetites.

The murder trial proved a tasty morsel, with the murderess quickly winning the sympathy of readers as she detailed the sordid love affair through the daily press. But McKinley was determined not to let the scandal have any effect on the day-to-day running of the government, and he was equally determined to protect Ida from any unpleasantness from the ordeal. Indeed, she bravely took to functioning as a White House hostess more so than before, clearly attempting to maintain a strong front for her husband.

When the trial finally ended with an acquittal for the murderess, Ida could no longer continue her performance and experienced the most severe epileptic seizures she had had in years. Hoping to cheer her up, McKinley took Ida to a peaceful resort on Lake Champlain, but his efforts failed. Next, he bought back their old honeymoon house in Canton and planned a railroad trip home to stay there. While giving a speech in Pittsburgh, however, a gun salute caused Ida to collapse. Finally back in Canton, McKinley summoned his old friend and political colleague, Mark Hanna, to an important meeting. Already the rumblings were being heard that it was time to consider another race for the White House.

"The way things are," a weary McKinley told Hanna, "the Republicans are going to have to find someone else. I can't expect to put Ida through any more." Hanna would not listen to any such notions. "But the country needs *you*. There isn't anyone else." McKinley shook his head. "There will always be someone else. For whatever pain the presidency of the United States may inflict, there will always be those willing to endure that pain."

Chapter 9

Pride, Possessions, and Power

The United States had changed drastically during the four years that William McKinley had occupied the White House. McKinley had changed, too. Often he thought back to that March morning in 1897 when he gave his first inaugural address. Then, he had been consumed with the goals of protecting the nation's business interests and building a strong and sound currency standard while pulling the people together into a proud, hard-working citizenry. His desires for the country did not extend beyond its boundaries. He only wanted to do what was best for the American people.

A SECOND TERM?

As the time approached for giving serious consideration to a second term, McKinley reviewed his years in office with considerable disdain. Not that the country was spinning out of control on some disastrous course — hardly. The nation was enjoying a rosy economic condition. The monetary system had been secured with the gold standard, employment was high, and Americans seemed to feel good about themselves.

As for the general public opinion about the country's chief executive, McKinley was the most popular man in the nation. Even those who had jeered most at the President for his reluctance to enter the Spanish conflict had forgotten those days long past. To a majority of people in the United States, President William McKinley symbolized a wise and effective leader who had strengthened the nation while at the same time reaching out and acquiring new lands and people.

Yet it was the latter realization that troubled McKinley deeply. Upon assuming office, he had hoped to promote a feeling of nationalism among Americans. "There is so much to do within our country," he had declared, "and I hope that I may be an instrument of God and a servant of the people in accomplishing useful and positive deeds." Clearly, McKinley's sights were centered on a more isolated America, a nation powerful within its own boundaries and worthy of imitation by other countries around the world.

Any man's dreams, even a man as powerful as the President of the United States, are changed by circumstances. As McKinley carefully surveyed the political terrain early in 1899, he recognized that while there was much of which he could be proud, the country was not the nation he had hoped to build. To Mark Hanna, his constant supporter, he confided, "There are some days when I wake up and I am very proud to be the elected leader of this great country. There are other days when I would be very happy to dispatch a messenger to William Jennings Bryan with an invitation to take over." It was a lighthearted remark at which Hanna guffawed aloud, only to look into the face of his weary friend and see it was not spoken in jest.

A Growing Imperialism

The crux of McKinley's dilemma revolved around the imperial power the United States had become in his first term of office. Somehow (and McKinley often wondered how it happened), the United States had acquired lands and territories far beyond its own boundaries. Filipinos, Japanese, Chinese, Malayans, Hawaiians, Spaniards, Polynesians, American Indians—all were living in territories now under the control of the United States government. How should they be governed? What rights should they have? What responsibilities?

The matter might have been simplified if all people under the control of the United States could enjoy the same freedoms and opportunities as did citizens living in New York, Utah, or Florida. But there were many Americans who did not want to turn all that the country had paid for in blood, sacrifice, and struggle over to strangers far away. As one senator noted:

> We, in America, won our liberties through a hard-fought revolution. We kept our Union together through the horror of a tragic civil conflict within our own borders. We have carved a powerful nation out of a wasteland, forever seeking a means to give every citizen a sense of personal worth and well being. Is this to be thrown upon people who cannot even spell the word 'America'? I would hope not!

McKinley heard this voice and many others. He was always willing to listen to the feelings of the people. And although he understood what the senator and others felt and were expressing, the President wondered just what *was* a fair way of treating those now under American domination. As if this question did not trouble McKinley enough, he was well aware there were many Americans, some in high governmental positions, who were eager to reach out and grab more countries, wherever potentially available. It was a game of acquisition, of power, and of domination. It was not a game McKinley enjoyed.

Nor did the man in the White House appreciate what

was happening to his wife. The attacks of epilepsy came more often, and there were those who spread rumors of insanity about the First Lady. Always known to treat women with the greatest respect, it was said McKinley ordered two visitors ejected from the executive mansion when he accidentally overheard them gossiping about "Mrs. McKinley's deranged state of behavior" and "the tragedy of the President having to personally waste his time with a lunatic."

The Reluctant Candidate

When Republican leaders visited McKinley in the late spring of 1899 in order to shore up his willingness to again be their party's standard-bearer in the forthcoming presidential election, they found a most reluctant candidate. "If what you gentlemen are saying implies that I am a candidate for renomination next year, I want to say to you that I would be the happiest man in America if I could go out of office in 1901, of course with the feeling that I had reasonably met the expectations of the people. I have had enough of it. Heaven knows! I have had all the honor there is in the place and responsibilities enough to kill any man." Republicans seated around their leader exchanged nervous glances. Could he really be meaning what he was saying? "There is only one condition upon which I would listen to such a suggestion," McKinley continued, "and that is, a perfectly clear and imperative call to duty." The tension in the air lessened just a bit. William would run if he felt the people wanted him to do so.

Dealing with the Colonies

Largely to show support for their political chieftain, Republicans began making a more concerted effort to get behind an open and free policy of international trade interests. Although McKinley had not openly sought American colonies scattered around the world, the colonies were there, nonetheless. It was only common sense to negotiate the best business dealings wherever possible. If America was to assume a pivotal role in world affairs, it was essential that such a position be financially beneficial. Through personal diplomatic contacts with representatives from other countries as well as public statements, McKinley let everyone know that the United States was always willing to "talk business" concerning exports and imports.

Recognizing the tremendous chore that lay ahead if they hoped to defeat the incumbent McKinley in the forthcoming presidential election of 1900, the Democrats planned their strategy early. Both the Senate and the House of Representatives were under Republican control, making the challengers' task that much more difficult, but the Democrats recognized that people are sometimes sympathetic to the underdog. Maybe this would be such a time. Carefully they looked for legislation sent from McKinley or backed by the House or Senate that could be used to convince the people "the Republicans are stuffing it down our throats and your throats."

The law calling for the President to administer civil government in the Philippines proved ideal. The Democrats tried to characterize McKinley as a power broker, thus rallying the imperialists behind their cause while at the same time soliciting the favor of the anti-imperialists by reminding the public that America was now occupied with matters far beyond its borders. "King McKinley" was one cry, and another Democratic voice asserted, "We've got problems enough here without taking on new ones across the sea."

Republicans saw through the Democratic tactics, but it was not an easy battle to wage. McKinley himself felt most uncomfortable. He knew he had to find someone to head the civil commission that would run the Philippine government, and yet he basically believed the United States should not be there in the first place. When McKinley invited Judge William Howard Taft to Washington to offer him the commission job, Taft did not waste words in expressing his viewpoint. "I am sorry we have the Philippines," the judge declared, "and I don't want them. I think you ought to have some man who is more in sympathy with the situation." McKinley shook his head. "You don't want them any less than I do," answered the President, "but we have got them and in dealing with them I think I can trust the man who didn't want them better than I can the man who did."

McKinley's complete candor and sincerity took Taft by surprise. As Taft continued talking to McKinley, the visiting judge became more and more impressed with the man on the opposite side of the desk. By the time the discussion ended, Taft had accepted the position. "I went under the influence of Mr. McKinley's personality," the Cincinnati judge revealed later, "the influence he had of making people do what they ought to do in the interest of public service." (Taft later went on to become the 27th President of the United States.)

PROBLEMS WITH PUERTO RICO

Although McKinley's experiences dealing with the Philippine Islands generally won him much respect, his actions with another United States possession, Puerto Rico, lost him considerable favor, even among his Republican followers. Since his earliest days in Congress, McKinley was closely identified with the protective tariff program, which was aimed at keeping American home business products secure by applying high import taxes on incoming goods. Because Puerto Rico was a territory of the United States, goods entering and leaving that island were not taxed. McKinley at first supported such free trade with Puerto Rico. But when some American business and government leaders suggested that "home industries" in the United States could suffer from no tariffs on Puerto Rican imports, McKinley reversed himself. His support helped pass a bill taxing goods imported from Puerto Rico.

Immediately Democrats accused the President of "flip-flopping" on the issue. "Apparently the man in the White House has forgotten that 'taxation without representation' was one of the major reasons for the United States breaking away from England," wrote one newspaper editor. "Puerto Rico has no voice in our government, and yet this country must pay taxes to our coffers. Woe to thee, Mr. McKinley." Republicans, too, were shocked at their leader's actions, which seemed to place economic interests above moral and constitutional principles. "The Constitution follows the flag," many periodicals headlined. "Has McKinley been listening to the voices of Big Business for too long?" other editors asked.

Still another ugly charge surfaced. Had the Republican action in taxing imports from Puerto Rico stemmed in any way from a feeling against blacks? Since Abraham Lincoln, the first Republican President, had written the Emancipation Proclamation in 1863, his party had been identified with the cause of freedom for all, regardless of race. Behind closed doors, there were now whispers of prejudice and bigotry (the belief that one race is better than another). Even the popular McKinley was among the accused. "A chameleon is said to be a reptile capable of turning colors to whatever situation he finds himself in," noted a spokesman from the Democratic camp of William Jennings Bryan, who was already marshalling his forces for another attack on McKinley. "It would appear that the man in the White House has a good deal of chameleon in him."

Secretary of State Problems

While McKinley felt the sting of criticism from Democrats and Republicans alike, the shrewd movements of one of his Cabinet appointees managed to cast a favorable spotlight on the entire administration. Secretary of State John Hay proved himself a first-class administrator, a figure to be reckoned with in world affairs. But in truth, the spotlight on Hay was brightened by the rather dismal performance of McKinley's first secretary of state, John Sherman.

Historians have speculated on why McKinley selected Sherman to fill the position of spokesman for the United States in the international arena. Perhaps it was a longtime personal loyalty and respect for a fellow Ohioan. McKinley put much stock in such things. Or maybe he remembered those moments when Sherman could hold those in a government chamber spellbound with his moving orations. There was no doubt that Sherman could be brilliant indeed.

But by the time John Sherman was appointed secretary of state in the McKinley administration, his days of triumph were over. Most attributed Sherman's ineptness to senility, gently excusing his errors and forgetfulness to old age. There was little doubt, however, that Sherman's mistakes carried the potential to cause major problems. He was constantly criticizing other countries through the American press, and McKinley was often called upon to explain and apologize. In April of 1898, while meeting with the Austrian foreign minister, Sherman suddenly discovered that he could not remember anything about American foreign policy; his mind went completely blank. At this point in time, the crisis with Cuba was reaching a climax, and McKinley could not risk any further troubles with his secretary of state. Sherman was asked to resign and did so. While McKinley pondered a replacement, an assistant filled in.

Enter John Hay. Few men were better known around Washington, D.C., than Hay, who, at age 22, came to the nation's capital to serve as private secretary for President Abraham Lincoln. After Lincoln's death, Hay moved to the State Department, where he became assistant secretary in 1878. Not only did he distinguish himself in governmental service, he also achieved prominence as a literary figure, publishing everything from ballads to analytical history. Having appointed Hay ambassador to England in 1897, McKinley recognized that he might be an able replacement for Sherman. It was a prudent move, and both men prospered in its execution. Hay officially took over as secretary of state in September of 1898. Soon it became clear that Hay was to leave an indelible mark on the pages of U.S. history, pulling the once-avowed isolationist, McKinley, onto the international stage of imperialism.

Chapter 10

A Door Opens in Asia

Compared to many other powerful nations scattered around the world, the United States was a relative newcomer in battling for international trade. Britain, France, Germany, and Russia were among those countries always on the lookout for developing broader bases of economic power, often seeking lands and people suitable for colonization. America, on the other hand, had turned away from such commitments, not wanting to become involved in the affairs of other nations.

When government officials from Great Britain suggested a discussion over possible trade arrangements with China during 1898, the United States showed no interest at first. "Our concerns are of a domestic nature," one State Department official responded. "We seek no additional responsibilities outside our country." That initial response was soon muffled, first by the events taking place in Cuba and the Philippines, and then by a realization that trade with China offered many opportunities. To ignore any trading possibilities would be cutting off economic growth. No sooner had John Hay taken over the reins of the State Department than America's attitude changed to "We're always willing to listen."

THE OPEN DOOR POLICY

The time for discussion, however, had passed. Like vultures swooping in for the kill, the English, Germans, Russians, French, and Japanese had already carved China into specific commercial regions and were developing the necessary transportation systems that would provide smooth trade routes. The Chinese central government, located in Peking (now called Beijing), was helpless against the outsiders who had come to make money off of the country's people. Leaders of the plundering nations even threatened to outlaw the collection of trade taxes by the Chinese government. Such action by outsiders would topple just about any kind of domestic government.

Secretary Hay and a key advisor, Alfred E. Hippisley, who had spent years working in a Chinese customhouse, skillfully put together a plan aimed at weakening the tight grip other nations had on the Chinese economic system. They devised an "Open Door Policy" that would prohibit one country from interfering with another's interests in China, but would allow the Chinese government to set fair taxes on trade. Moreover, there would be no discrimination between nations on harbor fees and the use of railroads.

With diplomatic flair and eloquence, McKinley made the Open Door Policy public, declaring that the United States was not "asking only the open door for ourselves, we are ready to accord the open door to others." It was a triumph of statesmanship, for any country openly defying the Open Door proposal would appear to be power-hungry. When no foreign nation stepped forward to defy the American doctrine, Hay shrewdly declared the Open Door Policy "final and definitive," thus guaranteeing the United States a negotiating position with Chinese officials.

Retaliation Against Foreigners

While countries outside China bickered and badgered about Chinese trade policies, internal problems within the giant Asian nation began to escalate. Chinese nationalists resented the presence of foreigners in their country, especially since so many of these visitors assumed an air of superiority. "They are guests in our homeland," observed one Chinese official, "and yet they treat us like their servants. The more hospitality we extend, the more hostility we receive."

One secret Chinese organization, known as the "Boxers" (a nickname applied because of their fighting techniques), ordered all foreigners out of China, with threats of death if the warning was ignored. "Kill Foreign Devils!" was at first merely a rallying cry, but soon the chant was put into action. Missionaries were the initial targets, being brutally hacked to death by Chinese swords and sabers. The German ambassador met his death the same way. Foreign businessmen and diplomats huddled behind barricaded walls in Peking. Cut off from the outside world, those under assault prayed for rescue while listening to the angry cries of mobs outside.

An international collection of troops was quickly organized, with McKinley summoning 5,000 American soldiers to join 13,000 from seven other nations. "Must we forever be lifting rifles to solve our problems?" the weary leader moaned. "Why can't we merely lift our voices, shout at each other, and then reconcile our differences without bloodshed?" But few seemed to be listening. With guns firing, the rescue force landed in China, fought its way to Peking, and freed the beseiged foreigners. Again, McKinley was given accolades for swift military action, and yet, it was unwanted praise.

As the first President of the United States, George Washington had established a policy of avoiding any involve-

In 1900 American troops joined with those from other countries in an attack against Boxer revolutionaries in Peking, China. Although successful, the action was one more hostile military encounter that deeply troubled President McKinley. (Library of Congress.)

ment by Americans in the affairs of other nations. Despite the subsequent concerns of John Adams, Thomas Jefferson, and other U.S. leaders that American lives and property were entitled to protection wherever they might be, McKinley still felt Washington's thinking was more sensible. Clearly, the actions taken by the United States in the Boxer Rebellion violated Washington's philosophy, and as a great admirer of the noble leader who is remembered as "the father of his country," McKinley was bothered by the experience.

Payment for "Intolerable Misbehavior"

The Chinese revolutionaries had no hopes of victory against the soldiers sent by the foreign powers, and the Boxer uprising was short-lived. The Chinese government was fined $333 million dollars for its "intolerable misbehavior," $25 million of which was to be paid the United States. However, unlike leaders in the other countries that had also sent troops, McKinley was not vindictive and sought no revenge. After all, it was a rebellion by only one segment of the entire Chinese population.

"Our declared aims," McKinley told Congress in 1900, "involved no war against the Chinese nation. We adhered to the legitimate office of rescuing the imperiled legation [the group of diplomats],obtained redress [money paid as punishment] for the wrongs already suffered, securing whenever possible the safety of American life and property in China, and preventing a spread of disorders or their recurrence."

A careful examination revealed that the $25 million due the United States was more than adequate for losses incurred in the Boxer Rebellion. Eighteen million dollars was returned to China. This generosity by the McKinley administration, coming on the heels of the Open Door Policy, convinced Chinese leaders that the United States was indeed interested in cementing relations. The refund from the United States was put into a fund designed to enable Chinese students to travel to America for an education, bringing back methods and means for improving the country.

CAMPAIGNiNG AGAIN

The mantle of presidential responsibility rested heavily on the shoulders of William McKinley. At one formal dinner, a political ally noticed McKinley looking particularly tired and depressed. "Can you not forget for an evening that you are the President?" The chief executive shook his head. "It is like asking a person who cannot see to forget he is blind. No, my friend, it is not a job one can cast off, even for a moment."

The death of Vice-President Garret Hobart on November 21, 1899, further added to McKinley's depression. Often Presidents and Vice-Presidents represent little more than a political balance, weighed by party leaders to provide the greatest potential number of votes in an election. But McKinley and Hobart were also personal friends, only a year apart in age, and shared many similar interests.

Hobart's death reminded McKinley of his own mortality, an awareness often forgotten when caught up in the rapid movement of major world affairs. "The presidency causes one to think in terms of what will happen next month or next year, as far as laws and policies are concerned," McKinley wrote to a friend. "The death of Vice-President Hobart reminded me that I may or may not be here to view the results of any executive action I might take."

Enter Teddy Roosevelt

By 1900, Republican leaders had persuaded McKinley that he, and only he, could guide the ship of state through another four years. But with Hobart's death, the vice-presidential position remained open to speculation. Many names were bandied about, but the governor of New York, Theodore Roosevelt, seemed to be the prime candidate, at least according to the Empire State's political boss, Tom Platt. "He's got a lot of life to him, Teddy has, a lot of life!" Too much life, if you asked McKinley's closest ally, Mark Hanna. "I don't think that fellow can sit still for two minutes," Hanna once remarked. John Hay thought the notion of Teddy Roosevelt as Vice-President was "mildly amusing." McKinley was not sure what to think.

Not that Teddy Roosevelt was a stranger to McKinley.

They had worked together in Republican circles for many years. When the Spanish-American conflict began, Roosevelt, who was serving as assistant secretary of the Navy, resigned his office, gathered together a team of fellow cowboys and society friends, and headed for Cuba. The group, known as the Rough Riders, captured America's admiration, displaying raw courage and considerable recklessness in the face of enemy guns and swords.

After his exploits on the battlefield, Roosevelt returned to his Navy job and personally helped make a hero out of Commodore George Dewey by sending him to the Philippines, where he outfought Spanish ships. For the past two years, Roosevelt had been serving as governor of New York. In truth, Platt wanted Roosevelt out of Albany so Platt could more easily control the state's political machinery. The brash, bespectacled Roosevelt was not always easy to keep in line. As for Roosevelt's personal wishes, he did not want the vice-presidential nomination under any circumstances.

The 1900 Republican Ticket

However, by the time the Republican National Convention convened in Philadelphia in the summer of 1900, Roosevelt had changed his mind. Why? The feelings of one man did much to alter his thinking. No, it was not William McKinley. According to Roosevelt's sources, McKinley would accept whomever the convention delegates selected to run with him. Roosevelt was delighted to learn that McKinley planned to use his second in command the same way he had used Garrett Hobart—as a trusted advisor and consultant. Hence, the Vice-President's job would have both power and responsibility. It would have to for Roosevelt; he was not one for idle talk or inaction.

The man who changed Roosevelt's mind was McKinley's confidant and chairman of the Republican National Committee, Mark Hanna. When Roosevelt had first been

The presidential campaign of 1900 paired two decidedly differ-
ent political figures on the Republican ticket—the refined Wil-
liam McKinley and the brash Theodore Roosevelt. No one
suspected that in less than a year after entering his second
term, McKinley would be dead and Roosevelt would be occupy-
ing the White House. (Library of Congress.)

summoned to Washington to talk about the possibility of running for the vice-presidency, Hanna had told him to his face,
"You're not fit for the job." And whenever Roosevelt's name
was subsequently brought up in party gatherings, Hanna spoke
against the idea. Finally, in desperation, Hanna told one
gathering that seemed to be swinging to Roosevelt's side,
"Don't any of you realize that there's only one life between
that madman and the presidency?" However, the more Hanna
spoke out against him, the more Roosevelt was tempted to
take the vice-presidential nomination if offered to him.

When the National Republican Convention adjourned
on June 21, 1900, it was indeed a McKinley-Roosevelt ticket
that would carry the party banner. Two weeks later, William

Jennings Bryan was tapped for a third time to lead the Democratic challenge, with a former Vice-President under Cleveland, Adlai Stevenson, chosen to run as Vice-President.

Once more, the race was on. But if Americans thought
McKinley would change his campaigning style, they were in
for a surprise. "It won before, didn't it?" McKinley quipped,
as he settled into the family home on North Market Street
in Canton and prepared to do political battle. Again the residence was heavily fortified with telephones so the President
could have instant contact with campaign leaders in all parts
of the country. While Roosevelt traveled across the nation,
rallying potential voters with spirited speeches, McKinley sat
at home with a comfortable awareness that Ida was again enjoying the quiet of Canton.

Much to Do

From the beginning, there was much to do. The Republican
National Convention had lasted only three days, and during
that time most of the delegates' attention was focused on the
selection of a vice-presidential candidate. Little attention had
been given to the Republican platform, which was sadly lack-
ing in substance. On the other hand, the platform offered by
the Democratic National Convention in Kansas City neatly
spelled out plans for national growth. Immediately, McKinley carefully analyzed the positions of his adversaries and
provided the Republican stance. It was a wise political move,
considering that the Republican platform had so little to offer the American people.

Bryan again attacked the currency issue, defending the
value of a silver standard as opposed to a gold standard. But
although he was a commanding orator, he lacked the ability
to understand the people's wishes. He hammered away at the
fact that American troops were still waging a war in the Philippines, but in truth, the number of soldiers was small and the
hostilities had trickled off to virtually nothing.

The Democratic challenger also attacked the power that big business had in the running of the government, claiming that "the people will get what Mark Hanna and his friends decide, and let no one think differently." It was a reasonable accusation and was, perhaps, the claim having the most credibility; business trusts were alive and thriving, largely benefiting Republicans. However, Bryan could not connect McKinley with any unethical or immoral behavior. To many, he was "Father McKinley," that kind and friendly fellow in the White House who loved God, his wife, his country, and the American people. Bryan's job was difficult at best.

The Front Porch Candidate

As for McKinley, from the front porch of his home in Canton, he talked to reporters and offered them lemonade. He spoke proudly of the Open Door Policy, of the prosperity of business domestically, and of the lively trade in exports. Plans were in the works for a canal through Panama, and he respectfully credited Secretary of State John Hay for his efforts on behalf of this project. (There was, of course, no doubt who had appointed Mr. Hay to his position!) Yes, there were still skirmishes in the Philippines, but peace was just around the corner and a democratic government would be installed. It was one of the prices the United States had to pay for reaching out to help less fortunate people in other countries.

As the campaigning continued, McKinley sensed that he had more than one major opponent to deal with in his race for the presidency. He became more worried about Mark Hanna than he was about William Jennings Bryan. As usual, Hanna wanted to be an active figure in the campaign, and as chairman of the Republican National Committee, it was his right. But more and more Republican leaders were urging McKinley to ask his longtime friend to stay out of the political spotlight. Wherever he went, Hanna carried with him the image of big business as well as the tainted reflection of a crude political boss. "Everywhere he goes, he wins votes for Bryan," Republican advisors told McKinley. "He just has to be drawn in a bit, held on a short leash."

Hoping that he could avoid any unpleasant confrontation, McKinley bided his time. But when Hanna announced he was going on a speaking tour of the West and Midwest, Bryan's stronghold, McKinley invited his old friend to Canton, where they talked politics. Hanna still made the trip, but his speeches were reserved and guarded, clearly peppered with McKinleyisms that people had grown to love. Roosevelt, too, proved himself an able campaigner, winning praise even from Hanna.

Cause for Concern

On his campaign tour in the summer of 1900, Hanna uncovered talk that gave him cause for concern. Although he was unable to learn the details, he heard rumors about plans to assassinate a number of chiefs of state. Ordinarily, such rumors would have been ignored; there was always such talk among the discontented. But in the past few years, anarchists had struck down Empress Elizabeth of Austria, President Carnot of France, and Premier del Castillo of Spain. Only one Secret Service agent was assigned to the President of the United States. When King Hubert of Italy was slain by an assassin on July 29, Hanna shared his fears with McKinley, urging his friend to take more precautions. "Why would anyone want to shoot me?" the chief executive answered. "I have no such enemies." The truth was that McKinley enjoyed giving his bodyguard the slip when they walked in Canton during the summer evenings.

On November 6, 1900, the voters went to the polls. The Republican ticket of McKinley-Roosevelt amassed a total of 7,207,923 votes, while the Democratic team of Bryan-Stevenson garnered 6,358,138 votes. It was the largest Republican majority since Grant's re-election victory in 1872.

Chapter 11

Act Two
Begins

The William McKinley who rose to take the solemn oath of office as President of the United States on the morning of Monday, March 4, 1901, was a different man from the one who had stood in the same place four years before. Physically, he was considerably lighter, for a nasty case of influenza earlier in the year had sapped much of his strength and stolen some 20 pounds from the portly figure always so neatly attired in formal dress. Few in the crowd that braved the steady rainfall knew of the President's serious illness, for he had occupied a sickbed only when absolutely necessary in fear that public knowledge of his sickness might be detrimental to the country.

But greater than any physical change was the attitude McKinley brought into the presidency as he began his second term. The previous four years had heightened his awareness of the importance of the task at hand. His actions and those of the United States government were felt around the world. America was truly an imperial power, with ties and treaties everywhere. There was no turning back to those times long ago when isolationism reigned.

ANOTHER FOUR YEARS

In clear, resonant tones, the newly inaugurated President shared his feelings with those standing under umbrellas. He asked the assembly for their patience and prayers, their determination and dedication, as the nation reached to fulfill its rightful destiny. Clearly, he wanted no more war, no more hostilities. If only democratic governments could be installed in those countries now flying the American flag, if fair and lasting international trade agreements could be negotiated, if the canal across the isthmus of Panama could be constructed and properly regulated, if American business could thrive in an equitable manner among owners and workers—there was so much the man at the podium hoped to accomplish.

Not that McKinley was totally disappointed with his administration's accomplishments during his first four-year term—hardly. He felt that the military actions that had stained the record of his first term could not have been avoided and were contained as swiftly as possible. The currency standard had been solidified and the Open Door Policy with China introduced: yes, there were positives indeed to take pride in as a new century opened.

But McKinley wanted Congress to take immediate action on curbing those business trusts which provided some individuals and some companies with unlimited wealth and power. There were some Americans who had climbed to the top of industry, constantly sharing their good fortune with workers and welcoming competition. Others, however, like McKinley's good friend, Mark Hanna, wanted no government regulations restricting their actions.

Also, McKinley hoped that Congress might take the lead in establishing fair reciprocal trade agreements. Seven times during his first term he had sent proposals to the Senate and House, each one outlining a treaty that would benefit commercial enterprise between the United States and other countries. Seven times the agreements had failed to pass. Such efforts were disappointing and frustrating.

A Cross-Country Mission

In an attempt to stir up public response on behalf of his programs that might force Congress to take action, McKinley planned a trip across the country. He knew the power of his speaking skills and the warm regard Americans had for him. If political action could not be achieved in one way, there were other methods that could be employed. He invited Secretary of State Hay to join him on the mission, but suggested that the majority of other administration officials remain in Washington. On the morning of April 29, 1901, a special train pulled out of the Washington depot carrying some 40 persons headed toward the West Coast.

By the time the presidential train arrived in California, McKinley was convinced the trip was a wise venture. Across the country, people had stood beside the train tracks, hoping to see their leader, perhaps to have him smile back at their waving and cheering. Even in parts of the South and West, normally reserved for Democratic favor, the crowds applauded his brief whistlestop speeches.

A special treat awaited the McKinleys in Los Angeles, where six white horses pulled a carriage covered with colorful flowers. "We wanted you to feel right at home," noted one of their gracious hosts. "We were told you and Mrs. McKinley have turned the White House conservatories into heavenly gardens, that every room in the President's home boasts giant bouquets." McKinley was pleased. "I had thought we had done quite well until I came here. Mrs. McKinley and I are most impressed."

But while Ida McKinley enjoyed the hospitality of all

those who welcomed her, she again fell victim to illness. A bone growth on her finger became inflamed and fever developed. The presidential schedule was altered so that she could rest in San Francisco for a few days. Doctors discovered a blood infection, and new treatments were begun.

As always, McKinley could think of little else other than his wife's condition. Business trusts, reciprocal trade agreements — how little they seemed to matter in comparison to his beloved mate's health! He did not hesitate cancelling speeches so that he could stay close to Ida's side. "I know I am disappointing many people," the chief executive confided to Hay. The secretary of state merely shook his head. "I think you have won the people's support anyway," he said.

Clearly, Hay was right. News of the President's concern for his wife reached into every home across America. The people were moved by their leader's total devotion to Ida. They sent letters of concern and support, promising their prayers. "I think we had better take another look at those treaties the President sent over," one congressman astutely told another. "With the mood of the country being as it is, I believe the people would give him anything he asked for right now."

Groundswell for a Third Term

The words rang true enough. McKinley's popularity was at an all-time high. Although he still looked back with sadness at the Spanish-American War, even those who had criticized him at the time referred to it as "a splendid little war," and credited McKinley with providing it.

But when McKinley heard there were those already talking about a third term, he was shocked. After all, he had scarcely begun serving his second! Wanting to squelch all possible thinking about the subject, McKinley issued a special statement to newspaper reporters on June 10. It was short and to the point.

I will say now, once and for all, expressing a long-settled conviction, that I not only am not and will not be a candidate for a third term, but would not accept a nomination for it if it were tendered me. My only ambition is to serve through my second term to the acceptance of my countrymen, whose generous confidence I so deeply appreciate, and then with them to do my duty in the ranks of private citizenship.

No one, not even McKinley's staunchest supporters, challenged his decision.

Summer's Tragic End

As the summer of 1901 wore on after McKinley's return to Washington, one day followed another in its heat and mugginess. Green grasses browned under a scorching sun, and everywhere people sought ways of escaping the heat. Because there were no urgent matters in Washington, McKinley gazed longingly toward Canton and scheduled time at home. Recovered from the trip West, Ida was, as always, cheered by the plans of returning to the family home. When they did so, the President became just another resident along North Market Street. He would pause to exchange lighthearted chitchat with neighbors during afternoon strolls and would play cards with local friends in the evening. The world of Washington, D.C., vanished while the small town of Canton, Ohio, nurtured its most important resident.

July slipped quietly into August. With each passing day, McKinley became more eager to renew the quest for public support that had been curtailed because of his wife's illness earlier in the year. With the help of his personal secretary, George Cortelyou, McKinley scanned incoming invitations that might offer the most opportune event for renewing his campaign to promote reciprocal trade agreements and limit business trusts. After all, the speeches were already prepared; now all they needed was the proper showcase.

At a reception on the evening of September 5, 1901, President William McKinley appeared comfortable and relaxed as he enjoyed the hospitality of his hosts and hostesses at the Pan American Exposition in Buffalo, New York. McKinley's personal secretary, George Cortelyou, seen here behind the President's left shoulder, had reservations about the next afternoon's activities. As it turned out, Cortelyou's apprehensions were with valid reason. (Library of Congress.)

After studying the plans and purpose of the Pan-American Exposition in Buffalo, New York, McKinley's mind was made up. "It's the ideal forum," he told his secretary. "Representatives of all the nations of the Americas will be there. It's a perfect opportunity." Cortelyou, ever cautious, promised to investigate the matter more carefully.

Within days, Cortelyou had checked out every aspect of the Buffalo event. Most of the plans for the President's two-day stay at the exhibition appeared satisfactory. Only a reception scheduled at the Temple of Music on September 6 posed a problem. The itinerary called for McKinley to greet visitors attending the exhibition. It was this time frame that most concerned Cortelyou. But, as usual, McKinley refused to listen. It was a tragic refusal.

Only a few minutes after McKinley had taken his place in the receiving line, a 28-year-old anarchist named Leon Czolgosz, once a worker in a Cleveland wire mill, entered the Temple of Music on the exhibition grounds. In his pocket he carried a .32-caliber revolver. Approaching McKinley, Czolgosz raised the gun and fired two shots. As stunned guards and onlookers wrestled Czolgosz to the floor, the 25th President of the United States collapsed.

Chapter 12

A World Mourns

The surgery on William McKinley took place in the emergency operating room on the grounds of the Pan-American Exhibition. Had there been more time, more care could have been taken with the operation. Of the two bullets fired, one fell out when the President's clothing was removed in preparation for the surgery. This was from the shot that had merely bruised his ribs. But the second bullet had passed through the abdomen. Had the doctors thought of it, they might have secured the X-ray machine on display at the exhibition, brought it to the first-aid station, located the bullet, and removed it. But everything had happened too fast.

Quickly the surgeons cleaned out the abdominal cavity and sewed up the wounds. They assumed the bullet had lodged in some back muscle tissue and would not cause further trouble. Following the surgery, McKinley was taken to the Milburn house, where the presidential party was staying. A worried Ida McKinley was waiting to comfort her spouse as he had so often cared for her.

A TRAGIC DEATH

McKinley had been shot on Friday afternoon, and throughout the weekend members of his administration flocked to Buffalo. But by Monday afternoon, McKinley had improved.

Vice-President Roosevelt and the other government officials who had rushed to Buffalo prepared to depart, satisfied the President was out of danger. Even Ida McKinley was coaxed into going for a drive, leaving her husband's bedside for the first time since he had been brought to the Milburn home after the shooting.

A Deadly Infection

An offer to bring X-ray machinery to the President's bedside was refused by the attending physicians. "It would simply be wasting time," one doctor flippantly commented. "The President shows every sign of making a complete recovery." To the naked eye, the physician's observation was totally correct. McKinley's color had returned, as well as his laughter. By the evening of September 10, he was sleeping comfortably. The following day, he smoked a cigar. But inside McKinley's body, deadly gangrene was spreading through his intestines, pancreas, and kidneys. No one could see that was happening.

On the morning of September 12, Dr. Charles McBurney, a noted abdominal specialist, arrived from New York City to examine McKinley and to talk to his doctors. Dr. McBurney heaped glowing praise on the attending physicians. "This is the climax of human skill," observed McBurney. "You have reached the supreme limit of science. No greater victory has ever been won. If this wound had been inflicted on a European sovereign, he would surely have died. I congratulate you."

Satisfied with their efforts, the various physicians made plans to return to their respective homes. But on the afternoon of September 12, trouble appeared. Receiving his first solid food since the surgery, McKinley showed signs of rejecting it. He was unable to digest anything. Quantities of castor oil were administered; heart stimulants were tried. Nothing worked. By nightfall, it was clear the President was dying.

Ida McKinley returned to her husband's bedside, leaned over and whispered a few private words. He smiled but did not speak. Administration officials who had been summoned also appeared, but the President showed no awareness of their presence. A sobbing Mrs. McKinley was helped from the room, to be replaced moments later by a pale, grim Mark Hanna. "Mr. President!" the old colleague said, his voice struggling to control itself. Hanna dropped to his knees beside the bed. "William, William," he pleaded, but McKinley did not respond.

Convinced the President was recovering, Roosevelt had gone to the Adirondack Mountains in New York. A telegram from Cortelyou—"The President's condition has greatly changed for the worse"—brought a shocked Vice-President hurrying back to Buffalo.

But he was too late. In the darkness of September 14, shortly after 2:00 A.M., William McKinley passed away.

Roosevelt Sworn In

It was early in the afternoon of the 14th before Roosevelt reached Buffalo. While administration officials tried to determine appropriate procedures for swearing in the new President, Roosevelt called upon Mrs. McKinley to share his personal sympathy. He then went into an adjoining room to take the oath of office as the 26th President of the United States. "It shall be my aim to continue absolutely unbroken the policy of President McKinley for the peace and prosperity and honor of our beloved country," Roosevelt promised. At 42 years old, he was the youngest man ever to become President.

A PRESIDENT EULOGIZED

News of McKinley's death traveled swiftly across the nation, bringing tears to those who had loved the man as well as to those who had attacked him. William Jennings Bryan, twice defeated by McKinley in presidential campaigns, labeled the martyred leader "a genius." Former President Grover Cleveland noted, "All our people loved their dead President. His kindly nature and lovable traits of character, and his amiable consideration for all about him will long live in the minds and hearts of his countrymen."

From other countries, too, came tributes. Typical of such eulogies was Canon Duckworth of England, who called McKinley's death "an unspeakable loss not only to his own country but to ourselves and, indeed, the whole world."

For five days, the country mourned. McKinley's body was returned to Washington, where the casket was placed in the Capitol rotunda. Thousands came to pay their respects. In major cities and small villages, flags were lowered to half-mast, church bells tolled sadly, and families gathered to share quiet conversation about "Father McKinley." There were those who had mourned before, when the bullets of assassins had cut down Abraham Lincoln and James Garfield. The question was pondered, "Why, in a nation founded with peace as a goal, should violence claim such good men?" It was a question no one could answer.

From Washington, the funeral train headed slowly back to Canton, where William McKinley would be buried. Along the railroad tracks people gathered quietly, in honor of their fallen leader. He was laid to rest on September 19 in a Canton cemetery, where his beloved wife, Ida, would join him some six years later.

An Assassin's Fate

As for the assassin, Leon Czolgosz, justice moved with unusual swiftness. He claimed to have acted totally alone in carrying out his deadly mission, and there was no reason to think differently. He admitted to being an anarchist, writing a simple statement of 25 words: "I killed President McKinley because I done my duty. I didn't believe one man should have so much service and another man should have none."

More than one who read Czolgosz's statement could not help but think that of all who would have been willing to try and help him, William McKinley would have been the first to offer. But all that was past; it was the present that required action.

Problems arose in the Czolgosz trial when no one could be found to defend him. It took the efforts of New York's Governor Benjamin Odell before two attorneys, Loran Lewis and Robert Titus, reluctantly accepted the task. Because the defendant did not believe in courts anyway, he made no attempts to help himself. No defense witnesses were called, and the jury found Czolgosz guilty one day after the trial opened. He was sentenced to death, and one month later, Leon Czolgosz was electrocuted in Auburn Prison.

THE LEGACY OF WILLIAM McKINLEY

Historians have never found it easy in "ranking" McKinley among the Presidents of the United States. Part of the problem comes from an awareness of the 25th chief executive as a person—an honest, virtuous man who reached out to anyone in need. His concern for his wife was legendary, but one might accept that devotion as to be expected. But how does one explain a man's concern for a person who has just fired two shots into his body and then orders nearby guards, "Don't let them hurt him!"? Truly, William McKinley possessed a genuine compassion for others that was beyond measurement. If personal feelings toward others were the only way to evaluate Presidents, McKinley would rank well indeed.

But when judging Presidents, other criteria must be employed—criteria which showed that McKinley lacked strength of leadership in times of crisis. Upon assuming office, he was warned by outgoing President Grover Cleveland of potential difficulties with Spain. One more skilled in international affairs might have prevented the Spanish-American War as well as the uprising in the Philippines. And so consumed was he with the value of high protective tariffs that McKinley recognized too late the worth of reciprocal trade agreements. In his final address to the American people, however (the one he gave at the Pan-American Exposition), McKinley showed that he understood the importance of working together with other nations for economic strength:

> The period of exclusiveness is past. The expansion of our trade and commerce is the pressing problem. Commercial wars are unprofitable. A policy of good will and friendly trade relations will prevent reprisals. Reciprocity treaties are in harmony with the spirit of the times; measures of retaliation are not . . . . Let us ever remember that our interest is in concord, not conflict; and that our real eminence rests in the victories of peace, not those of war.

Overall, McKinley was a President who sensed and followed the wishes of the people. Most historians would argue that great leadership reflects an individual's perceptive powers in analyzing the needs of his or her nation and acting forcefully and responsibly to execute those needs. Despite high marks earned by establishing a strong currency standard, an Open Door Policy with China, and the selection of key administrative personnel, McKinley was too often led by events as they occurred rather than initiating quality statesmanship. He could, perhaps, be rated as an average President.

Yet few men have provided a more distinguished personal legacy in character than did William McKinley. One history scholar who followed McKinley into the White House some four decades later perhaps summed up the situation best. "You might find a better leader," observed Harry S. Truman, "but you'd have to look a long way to find a better man."

Bibliography

Bailey, Thomas A. *The Pugnacious Presidents.* New York: The Free Press, 1980. A careful look at how William McKinley, a confirmed isolationalist, is persuaded by the times and the mood of the people toward imperialism.

Barclay, Barbara. *Lamps to Light the Way.* New York: Bowman, 1970. A brief but pleasurable glance at the Presidents (Washington through Nixon) which highlights the personal side as well as the public achievements of the country's chief executives.

Bassett, Margaret. *American Presidents and Their Wives.* Freeport, Maine: Bond Wheelright, 1969. McKinley's presidency takes back seat in this volume, which focuses instead on the man himself and his wife, Ida. Little has been written about Ida Saxton McKinley, and this book shares the warmth and concern that made their relationship unique.

Hoyt, Edwin P. *William McKinley.* Chicago: Reilly & Lee, 1967. This selection is one of several quality biographies authored by Hoyt. The biographer offers a penetrating look at William McKinley while analyzing the times of his presidency.

Kane, Joseph Nathan. *Facts About the Presidents.* New York: H. W. Wilson, 1981. From Washington to Reagan, Kane's authoritative compilation of facts and historical data is a prime source for presidential research.

Kent, Zachary. *William McKinley.* Chicago: Children's Press, 1988. One of the Encyclopedia of Presidents series aimed at upper elementary readers, this volume offers a quick, easy-to-read look at the entire life of William McKinley. Lively black and white photographs enhance the book.

Morgan, James. *Our Presidents.* New York: Macmillan, 1924. The writing style is a bit flowery, typical of the times in which the volume first appeared, but it has enjoyed countless reprintings because of its unique look at the nation's leaders through the mid-1920s.

Morris, Edmund. *The Rise of Theodore Roosevelt.* New York: Coward, McCann & Geoghegan, 1979. Although the main focus is upon William McKinley's Vice-President, this carefully detailed biography provides a fascinating look at both Roosevelt and his predecessor.

Weisberger, Bernard A. *Reaching for Empire.* Alexandria, Virginia: Time-Life Books, 1963. Covering the time frame of 1890–1901, this volume of the celebrated Time-Life series offers a look at the McKinley era and how it affected the entire nation. In words and pictures, it's a delightful look back into history.

Whitney, David C. *The American Presidents.* Garden City, New York: Doubleday, 1978. How did William McKinley come to the White House, and what did he achieve while he was there? This book has the answers, in a straight-forward, clear style.

Index

PRESIDENTS OF THE UNITED STATES

GEORGE WASHINGTON	L. Falkof	0-944483-19-4
JOHN ADAMS	R. Stefoff	0-944483-10-0
THOMAS JEFFERSON	R. Stefoff	0-944483-07-0
JAMES MADISON	B. Polikoff	0-944483-22-4
JAMES MONROE	R. Stefoff	0-944483-11-9
JOHN QUINCY ADAMS	M. Greenblatt	0-944483-21-6
ANDREW JACKSON	R. Stefoff	0-944483-08-9
MARTIN VAN BUREN	R. Ellis	0-944483-12-7
WILLIAM HENRY HARRISON	R. Stefoff	0-944483-54-2
JOHN TYLER	L. Falkof	0-944483-60-7
JAMES K. POLK	M. Greenblatt	0-944483-04-6
ZACHARY TAYLOR	D. Collins	0-944483-17-8
MILLARD FILLMORE	K. Law	0-944483-61-5
FRANKLIN PIERCE	F. Brown	0-944483-25-9
JAMES BUCHANAN	D. Collins	0-944483-62-3
ABRAHAM LINCOLN	R. Stefoff	0-944483-14-3
ANDREW JOHNSON	R. Stevens	0-944483-16-X
ULYSSES S. GRANT	L. Falkof	0-944483-02-X
RUTHERFORD B. HAYES	N. Robbins	0-944483-23-2
JAMES A. GARFIELD	F. Brown	0-944483-63-1
CHESTER A. ARTHUR	R. Stevens	0-944483-05-4
GROVER CLEVELAND	D. Collins	0-944483-01-1
BENJAMIN HARRISON	R. Stevens	0-944483-15-1
WILLIAM McKINLEY	D. Collins	0-944483-55-0
THEODORE ROOSEVELT	R. Stefoff	0-944483-09-7
WILLIAM H. TAFT	L. Falkof	0-944483-56-9
WOODROW WILSON	D. Collins	0-944483-18-6
WARREN G. HARDING	A. Canadeo	0-944483-64-X
CALVIN COOLIDGE	R. Stevens	0-944483-57-7

HERBERT C. HOOVER	B. Polikoff	0-944483-58-5
FRANKLIN D. ROOSEVELT	M. Greenblatt	0-944483-06-2
HARRY S. TRUMAN	D. Collins	0-944483-00-3
DWIGHT D. EISENHOWER	R. Ellis	0-944483-13-5
JOHN F. KENNEDY	L. Falkof	0-944483-03-8
LYNDON B. JOHNSON	L. Falkof	0-944483-20-8
RICHARD M. NIXON	R. Stefoff	0-944483-59-3
GERALD R. FORD	D. Collins	0-944483-65-8
JAMES E. CARTER	D. Richman	0-944483-24-0
RONALD W. REAGAN	N. Robbins	0-944483-66-6
GEORGE H.W. BUSH	R. Stefoff	0-944483-67-4

GARRETT EDUCATIONAL CORPORATION
130 EAST 13TH STREET
ADA, OK 74820